ON STAGE WITH KEVIN KLING

ON STAGE WITH
KEVIN KLING

Minnesota Historical
Society Press

For Dietz and Mike

www.mhspress.org

The Minnesota Historical Society Press is a member of the Association of American University Presses.

Manufactured in the United States of America

10 9 8 7 6 5 4 3 2 1

♾ The paper used in this publication meets the minimum requirements of the American National Standard for Information Sciences—Permanence for Printed Library Materials, ANSI Z39.48-1984.

Library of Congress Cataloging-in-Publication Data

Kling, Kevin, 1957–
   [Works. Selections]
   On stage with Kevin Kling / Kevin Kling.
      pages cm
   Summary: "A behind-the-scenes view of one of Minnesota's most popular storytellers. This volume contains the full text of three of Kevin Kling's stage pieces—*21A*, *The Ice Fishing Play*, and *Scarecrow on Fire*—as well as excerpts from *Of Mirth and Mischief*, *Back Home*, and *Gulliver Unravels*. Previously unpublished poems, short pieces, and a conversation between the Fitzgerald Theater's Tony Bol and the writer provide a window into Kling's creative and collaborative process" —Provided by publisher.
   ISBN 978-0-87351-916-8 (hardback)
   ISBN 978-0-87351-917-5 (ebook)
   I. Title.
   PS3561.L497A6 2013
   812'.54—dc23   2013036364

PUBLISHER'S NOTE

How does he do it? Tell stories so rooted in place, yet so universal in effect?

This book takes readers on stage and into the creative process with playwright and storyteller Kevin Kling, who has been writing and performing in Minnesota and around the country since the 1980s. In a thoughtful interview, Kling discusses the importance, the history, and the process of storytelling, emphasizing his connection to Minnesota. And it is in that connection to the "clay" of this place that Kling addresses, with deep humanity, the themes that transcend place: recognition, home, family, loss—and the importance of paying for your ride on the bus. Scripts for three of his major plays allow readers to experience productions that work both on the stage and on the page. A few stories and poems further demonstrate his versatility; photos from throughout his career leaven the mix and show him at work with talented collaborators.

We hope you enjoy this behind-the-scenes visit with a regional treasure whose insights into Minnesota culture have delighted audiences nationwide for decades.

CONTENTS

ON STAGE WITH KEVIN KLING

A STORY TOLD

Storyteller and humorist Kevin Kling and Tony Bol, director of performance programs at Minnesota Public Radio, met at MPR in St. Paul and spoke for an hour about the importance of storytelling, Kevin's career, and the collaboration between the artist and MPR for performances at the Fitzgerald Theater. This is an edited version of their conversation.

TB: So, Kevin! *A Story Told.* The time when people lean forward, and tune in, and listen in a different way. We certainly consume stories in lots of ways: we watch movies, we read books. But what happens to a story while it's being told in person? How does it come to life?

KK: There's a big difference between listening to a story told live and learning it some other way. Scientists can observe areas of your brain and see what parts light up when you're thinking about something, and they've shown that when you read a story, the information is processed in an isolated part of the brain. But when you're in the room with a storyteller, it's a visceral experience. The story comes through the eyes and ears and even chemically. If a storyteller talks about throwing a ball with his right arm, the area of your brain that throws a ball with the right arm lights up. So when you are told a story in person, the experience is actually *transferred* to you. I think there's a lot to that. In the world of storytelling, one of the crucial first pieces of advice you get is this: never memorize a story, never learn the *words* of a story. Learn the *imagery,* because that's what you're trying to pass on. You're trying to create a larger world inside the imagination of the person hearing or experiencing the story.

1

TB: When I see you tell a story, I never think you're acting. I always know that there will be surprises, things that are outside of the guided conversation, something new. You use your whole body, even your feet—and all of a sudden, your feet are doing something. I suspect that you're not even aware of your own feet, sometimes.

KK: No. I'm aware that my legs are tired when I'm done. My whole *body* is tired. When you're done telling a whole evening of stories, there isn't a part of you that isn't kind of going, *What? What just happened?*

TB: As you craft a story, in the very beginning, I imagine you make reference to storytellers who have inspired you. But do you first imagine a story by telling it aloud, or do you think through it in your head?

KK: It's all different. When I create a story, it comes from a lot of different places. One of my favorite storytellers, Hugh Lupton, says that when you tell a story that you've heard told, the person you heard it from sits on your right shoulder, and then the person they heard it from sits on their right shoulder, clear back to the original person who told that story.

There's a lot of solace that comes with that, when you're telling a story. They say that when you lose your place, you look up and to the right. You can explain that in psychological terms, but I think of it this way: you're looking up to that person that's on your shoulder, and you're going, "Hey, how does it go again?" It also makes you responsible to that person on your shoulder, responsible to the story. It puts you in line with the story, like the "begats" in the Bible. It puts you in a lineage, it puts you with your people.

I think stories ask our big questions: Where do we come from before life? Where do we go after life? What's funny? What's sacred? I think they ask those questions because by putting a story in the mouth of a teller, even if we don't find the answers, we know we're not alone. To *belong* is sometimes more important than actually finding an answer. To know we're in a group of people who question, we're in a family. To me, that lineage, that idea of family, of recognition, is at the heart of stories.

TB: I'm fascinated by the idea that a group of people becomes something closer, a community, by the very act of being in a room listening to a story.

KK: That's true, it works that way. And there's more to it. A while ago I saw a National Geographic special on how we became human. Professor Richard Leakey was describing what happened when the climate in Africa changed and the forests shrunk, and we had to leave the trees. We had to evolve into humans in order to do that. We had to walk on two feet, so we could travel and adapt. With our hands free, we could use tools, get access to more food. Our brains became bigger with a different diet, and we developed language to pass on knowledge, and we lived in communities. But there was more to this than just bipedalism, tools, and language. One of the skeletons they found was of a woman in her twenties who suffered from bone disease. In other words, she couldn't have survived that long, couldn't have kept up with the group, by herself. She had to have help, be carried when she had a leg fracture. Instead of leaving her, they knew she was a necessary part of their society. Leaky argues that besides walking on two feet, and tools, and language, one thing that makes us human is compassion.

I would take that another step, as a person with a disability, with a couple of disabilities—shoot, probably more disabilities than I even know! I know that words like "tolerance" and even "compassion" have short shelf lives. Even compassion comes in waves. But I found that the word "recognition" is stronger, it's here to stay. When we *recognize* each other, when I see myself in you and you in me, then I know that by helping you, I am really helping myself. Stories are a crucial way of discovering and maintaining recognition. How *do* you recognize? What *do* we have in common? How *are* we family? These are all parts of compassion.

> STORIES ARE A CRUCIAL WAY OF DISCOVERING AND MAINTAINING RECOGNITION. WHAT DO WE HAVE IN COMMON? HOW ARE WE FAMILY? THESE ARE ALL PARTS OF COMPASSION.

TB: I like the idea of connective tissues running through stories, tying us together. It seems obvious when you say it, but I never thought of it that way. Of course it's true that compassion has that value. And how do you learn, or how do you engage compassion? By telling stories, recognizing each other, getting people involved.

KK: It's even deeper. I think that knowledge is acquired, but wisdom is recognized. And the idea of knowing each other as family is something we have to recognize, an *ah-hah!* moment. It's not something we learn.

TB: When you're telling a story, you have a sense of connection, and that brings up a sense of humanity. But I'm also fascinated with the connections to old stories, with how our ancestors came together to tell stories—and what recognition storytelling gives to the people who have not been around for centuries. You often refer to Greek gods.

KK: My friend Bill Harley, a wonderful storyteller who's won a couple of Grammies, says it takes about ten thousand tellings to get a story right. I think he's right. There's a part of the process that just requires repetition and seeing what falls away and seeing what lasts. The Odyssey was told for probably six to eight hundred years before Homer ever got a hold of it. Grimms' Fairy Tales, who knows how long those were being told before the brothers wrote them down? So it's a real tried-and-true method, it's crucial to the process, and it produces stories that last.

There's a wonderful Celtic scholar who's passed on now, John O'Donahue, who asked, "If we come from clay, what kind of clay do we come from—a peaceful meadow or a craggy cliff?" Your clay determines your characteristics, determines this point of recognition in who you are. But when I go back to the really old stories that are speaking to my clay—well, Rumi, the Sufi poet from the 1200s, has that beautiful poem, "Before right doing and before wrong doing, there is a field, and I will meet you there." It's a love poem, but it also speaks to that place before our consciousness.

I work sometimes with the Interact Theater company, and a woman named Ingrid who has aphasia also works there. Aphasia is a condition that makes it very difficult for you to turn your thoughts into words. So when she speaks, she's very poetic, but she can also be very difficult to understand. One day, she told me that before her aphasia, she used to feel, "I think, therefore I am." But since her aphasia, she knows we come from a deeper place. Now she knows, "I am, therefore I think." I think language is just our feeble attempt at getting to that place. It's all we have. It's our tools, you know. It's using a bulldozer to do brain surgery, but it's the best we can do.

TB: There are people who are very committed to a true story, almost to journalistic reporting. Then there's fiction. But there's something in between, as well, which may just be memory being a little foggy—but what is the role of truth and fiction working together?

KK: Well, truth has a ring to it, and I try to stick with the truth, as wild as it can be. It can seem really weird and strange, but there is a *ring* to it. Good myths have that. Joseph Campbell said, "Myths are the dreams of our society." They carry truths that resonate throughout the society. We look at stories to find those truths within the truths. I think that's why storytelling has made a bit of a resurgence lately. In broadcast media, for example, news and commentary used to be two different things. But now opinion and news have grown very close together. These days, we expect our newscasters to have opinions. Therefore, the idea of the storyteller has taken on a deeper meaning. Now we need the truths within the truth. We seek in terms of myth, in terms of something deeper.

TB: There are more places for storytelling now, especially on public radio, like the storytelling events that The Moth [the venue for storytelling in New York City, now active across the country] sponsors at bars, and *This American Life* performances on stage. I'm impressed with the sophistication of the audience. Not so long ago, there wasn't enough respect for the audience. You'd say, "Oh no, I can't have an opinion. I must just list the facts." We now respect each other and respect that we are good communicators, and we trust audiences to know the difference between fact and opinion.

KK: It should always have been that way. I was lucky, I think. I always relied on the idea that I could challenge an audience. I think that's why they come to live theater. You can go to a lot of places to *not* be challenged. I mean, there's plenty of media out there: for television, the *job* is to entertain, with sitcoms and dramedies, and that's a wonderful thing. Then there are stand-up comedians, which storytellers are compared to a lot. I have a great deal of respect for stand-up comedians, but they use a joke to close a door. That's what they're aiming for, to get people to laugh. It's a form that relies on entertainment, which is really important.

But a storyteller *opens* a door with a joke. We use a joke to create a family, and we can then take it another step. Storytelling still has an onus: you have to establish trust. Most of the time when you're a storyteller, you're on someone else's turf. So you have to establish trust. Why are you here? Why should they trust you? You have to find a place in between teller and listener, a place where we can meet. It has to be a conversation. A lot of times I'm down in the

South, somewhere that is not my home. I vote differently than ninety percent of the audience—probably ninety-nine—and I have to find where we meet right away, so that they trust me, so that we can go places.

Theater is different because there's a voyeurism attached to it. The audience is looking through a wall. There's no expectation that what I see on stage is like my home, or that I should think it's real or true. Theater needs to seduce, more than gain trust.

TB: And humor is a way to establish trust. I hear you being referred to as a humorist.

KK: I like that. That's one of the few labels I like.

TB: I've always thought that a comic tells a story to build a joke, and a humorist tells a joke to build a story. You have always taken on the role of a humorist, and the humor is not what you're pointing at—it's the humorous *part* of what you're pointing at.

KK: That's a good point.

TB: You use humor in some stories that are ultimately heartbreaking. But to get everyone listening, to get everyone comfortable and feeling safe somehow, your introductions start with humor. Do you want to say a little bit more about how that works?

KK: It's part of the trust I talked about. The audience has to know who I am before we go somewhere less comfortable. Mark Twain is a prime example. People are always talking about how funny he was, but he was pretty biting. You had Hal Holbrook perform his Mark Twain show at the Fitzgerald a couple of years ago. Oh, my word. He doesn't hold back on the biting stuff, which is such a beautiful part of Twain.

The whole idea of a humorist is really an American form. I perform in a lot of international festivals, and being a humorist is truly an American form, which is just wonderful. I worked on that play at the Guthrie—*The Venetian Twins*. Our director was British, and our lead actor was an American. Our lead actor finally *got* what was going on. He said, "You've got to understand the difference between British humor and American humor. In England they laugh at funny pants, but Americans need to have somebody in the pants." I completely agree with that. That's what we do as humorists.

TB: In other words, we need our humor to be a little bit more literal, sometimes.

KK: Well, we need to know who it's coming from. That was part of the beauty of Twain—he really let us know where he was coming from, who it was, who's up there talking to us. Again, it has to do with that ability to trust. Who's up there? Do we trust this person?

You're contributing to this, too, Tony. Holbrook was at the Fitz for a reason—you've made the Fitzgerald a premier venue for storytelling. I'm thrilled about this. But what I especially like is that you are curious, and you bring in performers who don't make a fixed border between storytelling and other performances. You're playing with a shifting boundary. What's the elasticity of the boundary of storytelling? I'd love to hear how you think about that.

TB: Let me start pragmatically, at the beginning. First, Garrison Keillor's work guides this concept, coming from public radio, where the word is very important. Garrison is a literary figure, well spoken and thoughtful. He can convey simple ideas beautifully and complex ideas simply. He has sent us in that direction. In fact, he's the person behind naming the theater for F. Scott Fitzgerald. So it comes back to words and writing. When shows at the Fitzgerald Theater come together, they showcase well-crafted words, which means we work with a lot of authors and people who know how to write.

So it began as a stage for *a story told,* and we just decided to continue in that direction. Mind you, that works well because we're radio. But we want to challenge our productions at the theater, to be at the highest level of production, and still not lose the craft of storytelling. So we won't do a play that has confusing, overlapping dialogue or crucial visual pranks. That doesn't work so well. In fact, we sometimes ask a few people to "see" a whole show with their eyes shut. We want to see if they get a complete experience, and we frequently learn something from that. So the very practical nature of making *radio* out of a performance keeps us working as a stage for a story told. Even with our musical experiences, we try to enrich the narrative. We work on what would be normally considered the banter in between musical numbers, so that those words, too, contribute to the art of the entire performance. So even in the musical performance, we take that time out for that story being told.

KK: That goes back clear to the beginning of storytelling. Most storytellers throughout time have been associated with music, whether their own or some other form of music. There's a wonderful production on Broadway of Beowulf. He accompanied himself on the lyre. I'm thinking that was redundant—a liar on a lyre. [*laughter*] That use of music, I love that you do that.

TB: We like the use of texture, the emphasis on details that will improve the experience. In fact, our lighting designer, Mike Wong, just received a McKnight Fellowship. It's funny to think that a radio station has one of the best lighting designers in the state of Minnesota, and we're very proud of that. He's been doing a lot of shows.

KK: He is fantastic.

YOU SAID, "WELL, ALL THIS SILENT FILM FOOTAGE HAS BEEN RELEASED INTO THE PUBLIC DOMAIN. I THINK IT'D MAKE A GREAT RADIO SHOW."

TB: We really care that much about the experience of a story told. We know that stories are told in a variety of places: coffee shops, somebody's living room. Authors read at bookstores and libraries, The Moth's shows happen at bars. When we are doing something at the Fitzgerald Theater, we want to make sure that it's well crafted, and frequently that means we rehearse, practice it, rather than straight-out winging it. As you well know.

KK: That adds unseen layers to the radio. It's adding a mystery behind the speaker. I really am a firm believer in that.

I've got to tell the story about when you approached me for *Scarecrow on Fire.* You asked if I would do a piece on Oz. You are, hands down, the best namer, the best title maker, of anybody. *Scarecrow on Fire.* How do you beat that? I mean, it was just great. I go, "Why do you want me to do this, Tony?"

You said, "Well, all this silent film footage has been released into the public domain. So there's all this free silent film footage. I think it'd make a great radio show." [*laughter*] I *thought* I got what you meant, so I just said, "Okay, let's go for it." And it did, it totally *did* make a great radio show. I've learned to trust you, and when you say something like that, I know it's okay. There's something else at work here, one of those unseen things that works its way through the radio, through the story.

There are things that happen in a narrative, in the power of story—people say, how do you put your stories together? There is a form of telling and re-telling that creates an invisible thread that holds a story together. It's not a visual syllogism, like something you see on a page. It's not something that even makes *sense* on a page. It makes sense through the telling of a story. The prime example is the Odyssey. You try to read the Odyssey you go, "What? They just switched narrators, why did they do that? Why are they calling Odysseus something different every five minutes?" But when you *hear* it told, all that makes sense. The shifting, it's all done to reengage the ear, to keep you interested. Every time we hear a different name for Odysseus—the liar, or the crafty storyteller, or whatever—it's all to tell us, okay, this is what this story is about. The story is about him as this. When you read it? Big deal. But when you hear it, it comes alive.

TB: I'm curious about the audience. When we're making a show, we have sometimes placed up to sixteen microphones just on the audience, because we don't want just the loud laughs—we want to hear the smiles, the little shifts in movement. That's part of the DNA of how the story is being told, where people are reacting. I'm curious about when you know it's going well with your audience, and when it's not going well.

KK: If I have an evening of stories, I'll set it up like a football coach. A football coach will have maybe ten plays that he'll use right away, and then by seeing how the other team responds, he knows what the other team's defense is. I have a set group of stories I tell at the top, and by the audience's response, I know what kind of audience I have, generally. Did they laugh at that? Were they moved at this? How far can I go? Did they come with this story? If so, then I know, okay, I can challenge this group.

After that, it works pretty much like a conversation. You're sitting across a table from somebody, and they're clearly getting bored, so you shift it. You've got to keep engaging the audience. If they start to drift, then you have to switch it out. In a story, you have the power to do that. On the flip side, when it's going well, then you come to the fork in the road where you say: Do I give the audience more of what they want, or more of what they *don't* want, which is usually what they *really* want? They're telling you, by agreeing or by being vocal or being excited, "Take us where we don't want to go, take us. We're with you now, and we're letting you know that. Challenge us, because now we're on your side." Then you try to get them just to that point where it just bumps—just before the rollercoaster goes off the track.

TB: I've seen you do that. I've seen you do a show three nights in a row, and the audiences chuckle differently, they breathe differently, and I can see that your pacing and your momentum really changes to match. They really are an important cast member, when it comes to making a radio broadcast, and it's important for your interpretation of the story, but it is also for the listener. You could be telling a story in a studio, but having that audience actually reacting brings some kind of honesty to the storytelling.

KK: It's always different. It really is always different. Even the familiar things can switch up on you. I work a lot with Simone Perrin, a wonderful accordion player, amazing singer. We've done a lot of shows that have runs, at places like the Seattle Repertory Theater and the Cincinnati Playhouse, and we've toured a lot. But we call Saturday night *date night,* and we've got to be careful. On date night, you're sitting next to somebody and you're trying to make a good impression. If you really laugh at something that's kind of out of bounds, you've just betrayed something of yourself that might not go over well with your date. [*laughter*] We've learned that Saturday night is usually date night, and the audience will be a bit more suppressed. It's like performing for corporate functions. You don't want to laugh like a hyena in front of your boss, so there's usually a lid on it when it comes to these performances, or where audience members know each other, but not well. It can even be the fifth grade, you know, or insurance salesmen.

TB: The most hostile audience—did you ever have one?

KK: Oh, man, yeah, you know, that happens a lot.

TB: Really?

KK: Yeah, for all kinds of reasons. Not very long ago I *did* do an evening for insurance salesmen. It was on the night before the vote was going to happen on the Affordable Care Act—Obamacare. All these guys *knew* that the next day, their jobs were going to change, for the good or for the bad, but nothing was going to be the same. So I couldn't tell jokes, these guys weren't going to laugh. If I told a tragic story, they would all go out the window. I had to think of something, so I told love stories. [*laughter*] That was all I had in my pocket. Their hearts were right there. That's all I had, though.

My buddy Bil Lepp has by far the best story about a tough audience. You had him at the Fitz—he's won the West Virginia liar's contest five years in a row, and he's one of the best storytellers in the country right now. Bil and I were comparing horror stories. He did a residence home, and there were two people in the audience, one guy on oxygen who immediately fell asleep, and a woman in the third row who immediately decided she did not like him. So he was telling his stories, and she got up and went to the door. Well, it was too heavy for her to push, so he had to go and help her walk out of his show. [*laughter*] So I go, *Bil you win, that's it!* That's the best.

TB: Which brings me to the idea of collaboration. Storytellers work in different ways, and we've been exploring that at Minnesota Public Radio. You know, of course, the way Garrison tells his stories, in a monologue. He's in that moment with just a microphone. Then we've thought about how else can we work with the collaborative process, where maybe Kevin Kling has a story, and then you work with someone else to see what transformations might happen. You've done that now in working with Steve Kramer, front man for the Wallets, and you've done it with the singer and songwriter Mason Jennings. In fact, I couldn't tell where the dominant story was, when you and Mason were working, because you were so closely connected.

KK: On an evening of storytellers, you know your role in the evening. Am I the invitation to this evening? Am I the motor? Am I the closer? You all know you each have a job. Then, on top of that, is that chemistry that you just hope for. That's in any kind of performance, with a storyteller or musician, and when it truly does happen, you are greater than the sum of your parts. And the audience is part of that, too. They are *there* that night. They are contributing. Everything, the stories, the tellers, the audience, it comes together, and it is an unforgettable experience. It's something you'll remember for the rest of your life. When I go to those nights, I'm good for thirty stinkers. That's what you really hope will happen, that connection with the other person.

And sometimes there's something extra, something that's just beyond reach. I remember one time I was at a Robert Bly reading. He was doing this beautiful poem, and when he got done, the whole audience let out this big sigh. He stopped and said, "Did you understand that poem?" We all went, "No." He said, "I don't understand it either, and I was hoping somebody did. But you almost do, don't you?" We said, "Yeah, we almost do." And he goes, "I almost do, too." He put something out just beyond our grasp. We could reach it, but we couldn't quite grasp it. We all knew that at the same minute, and he did, too. Obviously I'll never forget it, because it was one of those experiences where we were all something greater than the moment we were in.

TB: That reminds me of the first time I ever saw you, at the Walker Art Center. So I'm going to ask you about old collaborations and then newer ones, up to the one that we're working on with *Gulliver Unravels*. You were in a group called Bad Jazz. I was a young man, and I didn't know who you were, I didn't know Loren Niemi, I didn't know Michael Sommers, and I didn't know what I was up for. When someone says, "It's a night of storytelling," you just kind of put your money down. I think someone literally talked me into going. [*laughter*]

KK: That's how most people got there.

TB: I was shocked at the transformational power. That may have been the moment when I realized that this is something I really care about. I knew I cared about stories, from public radio, and Garrison, and all that as a young kid, but that performance showed a new angle. Some of it was rather abstract, but it took you somewhere. What was that early collaboration like, with Bad Jazz?

KK: Well, it was in the eighties, and that was a time of political ideology. If you didn't get into the tent, it was your own fault. A lot of us couldn't get into the tent, so somehow, it was our fault. So we reacted and acted out. For most of us, that was in the form of performance art. Because of the prevailing ideology, we couldn't test the heart of society, but we could test the way we did things. So we attacked the form.

TB: Will you just give a quick overview of what Bad Jazz was? It was mixing performance art with stories, right?

KK: It was. It was performance art. Bad Jazz was Mike Sommers, Loren Niemi, and myself. We met in 1983, when we joined a circus—the Heart of the Beast's "Circle of Waters Circus" tour down the Mississippi—and our subtitle was "Three men playing to the best of their abilities." Which really was true, we were trying as hard as we could. We had successes and failures right there, in front of people, because for about eighty percent of the show, we didn't know what was going to happen. We came in with ideas, and we just threw it out there. The chance that one of us would get stitches was higher than in any other show that I've ever done. [*laughter*] The stage was always trashed at the end, *we were* always trashed at the end. We could never do two nights in a row, because the second night, we just were done in.

> WE CAME IN WITH IDEAS, AND WE JUST THREW IT OUT THERE. THE CHANCE THAT ONE OF US WOULD GET STITCHES WAS HIGHER THAN IN ANY OTHER SHOW THAT I'VE EVER DONE.

That was an exciting time. In the performance art of the day, that's when people were really challenging the form. There were a lot of banned performances and performances that caused picketing. By the end of the eighties, the NEA [National Endowment for the Arts] had instituted the Decency Clause. It reminded me of stories I used to read about Ireland, set at the turn of the nineteenth century. They never said, "Are you going to the play tonight?" They'd say, "Are you going to the riot?" —because that's what would happen. [*laughter*] That's how it felt sometimes, in that period. We were really stirring it up, and we were stirring it up on purpose, because we didn't fit in the tent. Bad Jazz was one of those groups that got to perform at the Walker a lot. That was a golden time. The three of us have maintained a wonderful friendship. I still work with both those guys a lot. But Bad Jazz—it's just not its time anymore.

TB: How did you first get onto a stage doing storytelling? Did you start in college, at Gustavus in St. Peter?

KK: Yeah, I was telling stories there, but I didn't really know it. After I graduated I was at a party at Patty Lynch's house, in the kitchen. She was the director at Brass Tacks Theater, and she said, "Do you want to do that on stage?" I said, "What?" She goes, "What you did in the kitchen." Jim Stowell was in the kitchen, too. So we ended up on stage, just doing what we did in the kitchen, including drinking beer—which I've cut from this show. [laughter]

TB: I love the idea of "What You Did in the Kitchen." That's actually the title . . .

KK: Oh, no—see, The Title Maker!

TB: So after the kitchen—tell us about some other plays and other presentations for the stage, just a quick synopsis.

KK: Oh, man! There's been dozens and dozens. 21A is the one that got me out of the blocks. That came from the same place Bad Jazz did, that circus tour down the Mississippi. Mike Sommers and I would invent these characters the whole way, and after a while I thought, these characters are just too hilarious, I've got to put them on stage. I put them on a bus, all these characters on a bus. That bus went around the world. I could write a book about that crazy trip—Australia, Czechoslovakia, Sweden, England, lots of places. In Minnesota, it was a comedy, but in Sweden, it became an anthem for socialism—in 1987 Czechoslovakia, the oppression of the masses—I never knew what the response would be.

From there, I started writing plays—*Lloyd's Prayer, The Education of Walter Kaufman,* and the plays in this book—and doing some adaptations and children's plays, like Goldoni's *The Venetian Twins,* with Michael Bogdonov, for the Guthrie, and Kevin Henke's *Lilly's Purple Plastic Purse* and *Mississippi Panorama* for the Children's Theater. Luckily, I got hooked up with the Playwrights' Center in the mid-eighties, then Quicksilver Stage, Mixed Blood Theater, Illusion, the Jungle, and then the Sundance Institute and on to Actor's Theater of Louisville, and they produced a lot of my earlier works. In those days, that was really the launching pad to regional theater, and Off Broadway, and Broadway. I just happened upon these amazing places that were producing new works. In the early nineties, I did some work with Seattle Rep. And the Guthrie Theater has been so supportive. Joe Dowling—coming from Ireland, again, where storytelling was just part of the fabric of the place—he sought out storytellers. I couldn't believe it. He said, come on, I want you to be part of this building.

TB: You do *Stories from the Charred Underbelly of the Yule Log* there every year.

KK: I've done that at the Guthrie every December since the mid-nineties, one show a year. I did a tour with the Guthrie called *Freezing Paradise,* all Minnesota stuff. We were driving through Hibbing in the middle of February, and there was a big sign announcing "THE GUTHRIE THEATER PRESENTS KEVIN KLING." The February wind had blown the "P" away, so this big lit-up sign said, "THE GUTHRIE THEATER RESENTS KEVIN KLING." [*laughter*]

The Guthrie has just been wonderful. It's unusual for a theater of that caliber and size to support storytelling. My friend Bill Harley really said it well. Storytelling isn't the art form that will fill the Meadowlands, but it's the *seed art* that fills the Meadowlands. It's where it comes from. It's the form that starts it.

TB: I went to The Moth with Jeremy Cohen of the Playwrights Center, and he was telling me that a storyteller can say something in five minutes that provides exactly what the playwright needs to make a play. His people are listening to all kinds of public radio and going to listen where stories happen in the streets.

KK: You can get inspiration from anywhere, you just have to be paying attention. And it helps to be working with good people.

TB: In your storytelling, in your playwrighting, you've always done collaborations. You're doing one with us at Minnesota Public Radio now. We call it an original works residency, a three-year residency that will go to four or five, if we feel like it. We actually did *Scarecrow on Fire* before the residency started.

KK: Oh, that's right.

TB: Yeah, so who's counting? [*laughter*] But within the original works workshop, you've traveled around the state, this year with Dan Chouinard. What's your Dan Chouinard collaboration story?

KK: Oh, man. Dan is known in town as an amazing musician, which he is. He can play anything. We don't even *say* we're switching keys, you can just switch keys and he's right there. So most of us know him as a musician. A lot of musicians will play something, something they know, and the story sits on top of it. But there's a really rare musician who can *underscore* a story—actually get into the heart of the story as it's happening. And Dan is one of those few people. What he can do with a story, like in his work with Patricia Hampl, is just incredible. But his work at the Fitz and elsewhere— especially his Café Europa stories—shows his ability to tell a story and his ability to craft a story. So when we toured the state, I got to work with him both as a musician *and* as a storyteller. Because of that—he let me play my harmonica! [*laughter*] We went to Duluth, Grand Forks, and Rochester, and it went gangbusters.

YOU CAN GET INSPIRATION FROM ANYWHERE, YOU JUST HAVE TO BE PAYING ATTENTION. AND IT HELPS TO BE WORKING WITH GOOD PEOPLE.

There's something to be said for performing in different parts of the state. There's also something to be said for bringing people the stories of their own region. I remember when we toured *The Gales of November* [based on *Ten November,* the play Steven Dietz wrote set to music by Eric Peltoniemi, about the sinking of the *Edmund Fitzgerald*]. It was storytelling, but man, it's different when our own people are of legendary status. Lake Superior has one-tenth of the *entire world's* freshwater supply. And as it says in the play, "We didn't find the bottom until fifteen years after we walked on the moon." It has legendary status just sitting there. And we live by that lake.

The things that have happened in this state, on this clay that we live on, are worthy of legend. I think that's why Garrison surprised so many people when he started out. Southerners, obviously and evidently, embrace their eccentricities. Their storytelling has just been *thick* down there. But when Garrison started his work, people found out, *Wait a minute, they can tell stories in the North. Not only that, they're great stories. Not only that, they're as weird as we are. These guys are as messed up as anybody.*

TB: Comforting.

KK: It is really comforting that we don't have to live to such high expectations. [*laughter*] So I think that he opened up that door, but at the same time, the clay was always here. The stories were always here.

TB: In your residency, you've done two collaborations with musicians, *Of Mirth and Mischief* with Steve Kramer and *Back Home* with Mason Jennings. And for house bands, we drew on our rock service, the Current, for music, so we weren't repeating the traditional musical theater environment that's around the Twin Cities. You've worked with rockers from the band Halloween, Alaska, and with Abby Wolf and Haley Bonar. There's such a beautiful collaborative energy, it's just a different electricity that I haven't had in a long time. Everyone loves working with your stories, because you've always had a rocker's energy to your storytelling. You're willing to play beautifully with the absurd and kind of go at any pace.

KK: Thanks, Tony. Again, it's largely due to the chemistry of the collaborators— and I'm always curious to hear who you feel will be best suited for our next project. You never quite go "on the nose," like they say.

TB: I always like to create a little discomfort, because that's part of the creative process. Like costuming for the *Mirth* photo shoot. I could just point to it: there's the elf outfit. *Tights*, you've got to wear *tights*.

KK: I'll go in kicking and screaming, but I go in [*makes a dubious face*].

TB: That's it right there, that's the face. [*laughter*]

KK: My legs aren't made for tights. My friend Buffy Sedlachek says my knees look like I'm smuggling walnuts.

TB: Well, we were a burlesque house, and I've tried to honor that.

KK: I know. You're usually right. That's the sad part. [*laughter*] You've got a very keen sense of what works. I know from experience to just do it.

TB: We're working together now on a new project, *Gulliver Unravels.* That's one of the old stories—Jonathan Swift's parody of travel narratives, written early in the 1700s—that's stayed with you. Can you describe that inspiration for you?

KK: Well, it's one of those stories that keeps tugging at my pant leg. When I tell a story, there's always all these obvious parts, then there's the part of a story that goes, "I want to be in this, I want to be in this story." But even if it doesn't seem to fit, it doesn't belong, I've learned over time to really listen, because that's usually what the story is really about, and I just don't yet know why.

Gulliver is that in my life, and I need to tell it to figure out why. I think I'm getting really close. Like with Robert Bly, it's just beyond my grasp. There's always what a story *seems like* it's about and what it's *really* about. Gulliver has this incredible tall-tale quality to it. Most people just focus on Lilliput, where he's a giant and everyone's little. Well, in Brobdingnag, the second place he goes, he's little and everyone's a giant. In the third place, the scientists are floating in the air. The fourth place he goes, he decides to live with the horses, who rule the humans, who are called Yahoos.

The more I study this, the more it looks like the four stages of being a person. You are never more of a giant than when you're a baby. Everyone's at your beck and call and terrified of what you're going to do next. You are never smaller than in junior high and high school, and everything you do says, "Hey, I'm over here, I'm over here." In middle age, we're the clueless scientists, trying to fix everything and everyone. We think we're smarter than anything. Then the fourth stage, being with the horses, besides looking at what louts humans can be, that's also a return to nature, that serenity and senility that comes with age that takes us out. So the four places that Gulliver goes are really the four places we go in life. I want to explore that on those terms.

I also just love satire. And Jonathan Swift is Irish, and that's my clay, I'm going back to my clay. I'm really trying to embrace my tradition, back when my people were native, and that would be Ireland. So I really am fascinated on all those levels, but I know there's more, and I'm going to find it out in front of people.

TB: Talk a little bit about your writing process. Do you have any rituals or tricks to keep yourself going?

KK: My muse really kicks into gear under deadlines, and I am under a deadline a lot. But the really great ideas come at quiet moments, where it's a surprise. Because of my schedule, the only time I have real quiet is when I'm asleep. So I'll wake up in the night and then there will be an idea. It just needed me to relax before it could come to the surface. So I do generally wake up with a lot of my ideas. But those deadlines can come fast. About a week before the show, I'll say, "We've got to call Tony tomorrow and tell him we've got to cancel."

TB: Two in the morning is not always friendly.

KK: Every artist is like that, I think. You're always panicking. The worst was after my motorcycle accident in 2001, when I was still in the hospital. I wanted to find out if I could still write, and that's where "Bird Opera" came from. I was worried about crows appearing in my dreams, because I know they can be harbingers of doom associated with the underworld, until my pal Jaime said, "Crows take away things we don't want, so the next time they appear, load 'em up with your fear and send it away."

But I had a lot of fun with the process on *The Ice Fishing Play*, because I love to ice fish. So I'd sit at my desk pretending to fish. I made the rule: I'm going to sit in an ice house, in my mind, and no matter who comes to the door, I'm going to let them in. That's how I wrote that play.

The first two to come to the door were Mormons. They came to an ice house in the middle of the lake. I was pretty surprised, but I figured, okay, they're there, I've got to let them in. So these Mormons started talking, and they were the crucial element and the big question of the play. What are we doing here? What's going on? They asked the big question. It turned out that everybody who visited the ice house was somebody who had passed away in this guy's life. The Mormons opened the door for that to happen. I had no idea, I just went, *Okay, I said they could come in.* I didn't even know the people were dead until the end of the first act, and then, *Oh, wait a minute,* I started to figure out what the play was about.

When you're ice fishing, you're in a mythical land, and anything can happen on the ice. So that play really came from questions that were deeper than my conscious mind. In order to do that, I had to put myself in a place where my subconscious could knock on the door . . . And also, there was a deadline.

TB: What about writing for your collaborations for the Fitz? When you're collaborating, that's not a quiet place. You've got to work with another artist, go back and forth, like playing tennis.

KK: But writing is just another kind of collaboration. I think that anybody who writes characters *is* dealing with somebody else, because when the writing is going really well, you can't tell another person what to say. They have to tell you what they're saying. Really. You're taking dictation from the character. So I would argue that it's still a collaborative process. It's just collaborating with characters that are in your mind. A lot of times, a character will use vocabulary that I don't even have. So I have to rely on that. Or a character will be an age that I'm not. In order to be truthful to that age, I've got to let that character do the talking. Does that make sense? Okay, if I come across like a nut, I guess I can't help it. [*laughter*]

There's another way to think of it. David Abram tells this great story in *Becoming Animal.* He talks about being in the woods someplace where he doesn't think anyone has ever been before. He's so excited, because he thinks, this is something no one has ever seen. Then he realizes by the size of his footprint, the forest knows how big his foot is. By its indentation in the moss, it knows how heavy he is. By its direction, it knows which way he's going, and by the twig he snaps, how tall he is. Then he realizes, he's not exploring, he's being explored. I think that's what happens when you write or tell stories: you are both exploring and being explored.

TB: You have another great perspective on what happens in storytelling, about having a foot in two worlds. You had this experience literally, with your motorcycle accident, and you also talk about it in terms of storytelling and what the fool does. A reference to this, to how we endure change, is at the end of *Scarecrow,* and that was one of the finest endings I've ever heard in my life. Can you talk about that?

KK: Oh, man, I can talk at length about this. In mythology and folk tales, whether it's Odysseus, or Coyote, or Prometheus, or any mythic trickster, tricksters are hungry. Gods generally don't lie, because they're not hungry. This insatiable hunger creates the need to tell stories. So tricksters throughout time, and storytellers, have this need, this hunger, to tell stories.

And then there are fools. A fool isn't necessarily a trickster, and the fool has a foot in two worlds. The wise fool, like Nazrudin from Sufi lore, would be an example of that. Wise fools give pearls of wisdom, maybe accidentally or maybe not. Shakespeare's fool in *King Lear* seems to be talking gibberish, but he gives Lear amazing advice. He has a foot in two worlds.

Clowns are one step further removed. They have two feet in another world. So you can learn a lot by watching a clown, but you would never take a clown's

> I MADE THE RULE: I'M GOING TO SIT IN AN ICE HOUSE, IN MY MIND, AND NO MATTER WHO COMES TO THE DOOR, I'M GOING TO LET THEM IN.

advice. In the storytelling world, these would be the liars, the tall-tale tellers. So we've got the tricksters, and the fools, and the clowns. I try to be like the fool. I try to have a foot in two worlds.

Part of that has to do with my being in a motorcycle accident in 2001, and seeing that other world. But even more important is my left arm. I think my left arm is the reason I'm a storyteller. It's because when I was a kid, I could tell by the way people talked to me, by the way they talked *about* me, that I was on the fringe, I was not quite in the tent. Adults would call my arm "withered" or "crippled" or say, "you poor thing" or "what happened?" By the words they chose, I could tell whether they blamed me, my parents, God, or themselves for my condition. I could tell by the words they used what they were after, or what they thought of me. With that information, I could get what I needed from them. I was already working with rhetoric. Once somebody has an opinion of you, you already have them.

TB: And you are saying that they're setting your stage. Then you would know how to respond. The storytelling experience comes from how you reacted to that. But now you're an adult, and you go into schools or other places, and you still have people reacting to your left arm. How is it different, or how do you perceive it differently?

KK: Well, it depends. If I'm with kids, I address it directly, right away. Get it out of the way, and then it's not a problem. With adults, it's going to be a problem the whole time, no matter what, so I just leave it a problem. [*laughter*] I let them guess. It keeps them with me, you know, so it works just the opposite.

TB: Didn't you tell me there was a small boy in Thailand who they call the Little Kevin Kling?

KK: Yeah, they called him Little Kevin. I'm going to finally get to meet Little Kevin next January. He has the same congenital birth defect. A lot of people have arms like this. I love it when kids come up after shows. I always tell them they can come up, and they can't high-five me, because I don't have five fingers, but I have four, so we can high-four all day. So I get kids coming up, and whether they have five or four fingers, they get in line. They high whatever-they've-got me. [*laughter*]

TB: That's a moment of solidarity.

KK: You know, there are so many amazing storytellers for children out there. I don't think I'm one of them, so I go in kicking and screaming when I do kids' shows. But they are so rewarding. Then, when a kid who has a disability comes up afterwards—all of a sudden, you know, one of their posse is on stage. Then I know, *Okay, I've got to get off my stupid idea.*

TB: I have one last question: why have you stayed here, in the Twin Cities, and not moved to New York or Los Angeles? Is it that the region's stories are *your* stories, too?

KK: That's a good part of it. This is a very personal thing. I want to feel *necessary* in my community. I want to be as necessary as a plumber. What does that mean, for a storyteller? A lot of people get into acting, into theater and into stories, thinking they'll find that connection, but it isn't automatically part of it. You end up in New York or you end up in LA, and there's a great deal of yourself that's missing something. I think that's also why so many storytellers and actors go into the seminary or go into teaching, because they thought that's what acting was going to be.

But it isn't. You can find it, if you're lucky, when you immerse yourself in a community and become part of a community. You look around, there's so many artists in this area. A friend of mine from Australia came to the Twin Cities to set up a show, and she was worried about being able to come up with a choir, because not all places have them. We said, "What kind of a choir do you want? We've got girls', boys', women's, men's, gay men's, gospel, Lutheran, barbershop, Elizabethan, Gregorian, orchestral"—she was just floored.

One of the beauties of working here is that I can work with world-class performers and writers, musicians, composers, dancers, just in this town, because they're here *on purpose*. They've stayed here because there's something that feeds our creative energy here, something in our clay, in the legends of this place. Even more important, it fulfills our need to belong, to have a sense of family, to recognize and be recognized. It's home.

STAR ONE

FROM *BACK HOME*

My earliest recollection places me on my father's knee. He's pointing to the stars. "See that star?"

I reach out my hand. "Gaaaa."

Dad laughs. "You want to hold it?"

"Gaaaa."

"No," he says, "let's leave it there. You see, with that star, you can navigate the world. That star can lead you to places never seen by another, but more importantly, that star can take you home again."

"Gaaaa."

Had my infant tongue been more adept, I could have explained to him, "The universe isn't a machine, Father, it's a brain, a creator, that's why our lives are stories and not syllogisms. I have no intention of using that star as a vector. No, I want to *go* there.

"And if I can get to that star, it's a short hop to the next, and to the next, and in no time, I'm hunting with Orion, cart-wheeling the night sky with Cassiopeia, trafficking with heroes, drinking their wine, eating their meat.

"No, get me to that star, Father, and I'm never coming home.

"Gaaaa."

RAINSTORM, BRAINSTORM

FROM *BACK HOME*

After the storm,
after the rains stopped and the waters subsided,
wet but alive, the animals wandered
back into the forest, the desert, the mountain,
and seemed to forget about the time we'd spent together.

But *we* wanted to talk about it.
Let's do that again, that was incredible!

So we told it and painted it and danced it,
and by re-creating beauty, we created another kind of beauty.
If it could tell us what we know, maybe it could tell us what we don't know,
where we come from, where we go, what is funny, what is sacred.
Even if we never found answers, we knew we weren't alone.
Sometimes that was enough.
We began to traffic in the alphabet.
We imagined ourselves,
bragged about our opposable thumbs,
our heightened sense of self.
If we were made in the Creator's image, then we, too, could create.
If our dreams could surprise and delight us, maybe our work would surprise
    and delight the Creator.

We imagined ourselves to be in charge.
Our shared triumphs, desires, despair, connected us,
we recognized each other.
And to remind ourselves of love, of beauty, of truth,
we created ritual.
At times, it brought us together.
Other times, it was subversive, it was visceral,
it cut us from the herd.
Always it sought to take us somewhere before the song, the symbols,
    the myth.
That place before wrong, before right,
before the emotion,
that place where *I am therefore I think*—
to the white hot,
the birthplace of the sparks—
and then, it started to rain.

Kling, at left, as Jumbly Number Two in a performance of "The Owl and the Pussycat," Gustavus Adolphus College, St. Peter, Minnesota, 1976.

A postcard promoting "Under the Missletoe with Bad Jazz," presented by Quicksilver Stage in 1980: Michael Sommers, Kling, Loren Niemi.

Kling telling "Fishin' with Ron," which he calls "a true fishing story, probably the greatest fishing story ever told," during the Heart of the Beast Theater's "Circle of Waters Circus" tour, 1983.

The circus cast performs "Walter's Walk," a dance of fishes. Left to right: Mark John, Steven Epp, Marie Olofsdotter, Susan Haas, Kling, Doug Cain, Esther Ouray.

A postcard advertising Kling's first storytelling gig, "Gravity vs. Levity": Kling (left) and Jim Stowell.

As Buddy Layman in *The Diviners*, a play by Jim Leonard Jr. produced at the Chimera Theater, 1985.

Kevin Kling   James J. Lawless

SHORT STORIES
AND TALL TALES

30 July - 31 August 1986

Hennepin Center for the Arts
Little Theatre - 2nd Floor
528 Hennepin Avenue

Promotional postcard for "Short Stories and Tall Tales: A Portrait of an American Storyteller"
by John Olive, commissioned by ArtReach. The play was later known as "The Voice of the Prairie."

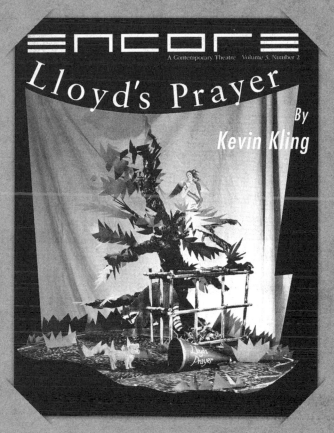

ENCORE
A Contemporary Theatre   Volume 3, Number 2

Lloyd's Prayer
By
Kevin Kling

The program for "Lloyd's Prayer," a parable about a boy raised by raccoons, produced in 1990 at ACT (A Contemporary Theater) in Seattle. It was developed at the Sundance Institute Playwright's Laboratory in 1987.

Kling as Bob the raccoon boy in the 1989 production of "Lloyd's Prayer" at the Illusion Theater. (ROBIN MACGREGOR)

TATTLER

By Jaime Meyer

Lee Blessing's play WAR OF THE ROSES will be performed in the Humana New Play Festival of Actor's Theatre of Louisville in March. It was read in July at the O'Neill. Lee is currently working on two teleplays commissioned by Public Television stations in St. Paul and Lincoln, Nebraska, and on a new play commissioned by Park Square Theatre in St. Paul, for production there in August '85 . . . *Marisha Chamberlain* is a recipient of a 1985 Rockefeller Fellowship in Playwrighting, and, along with *Patty Lynch*, has been invited to American Place Theatre in February for the Midwest Voices Project. Marisha is working on a new play commissioned by Theatre Three for production in Mpls. in August '85 . . . *Leslie Brody's* play EMMA ROTHSTEIN, in a production by The New Classic Theatre, played to sold out houses in December, and has been optioned for an off-Broadway production. Leslie is at work on a play commissioned by The Great North American History Theatre, a Western with a working title of QUIET, WYATT!! . . . *John Richardson's* play BROTHERHOOD opened Feb. 15 at Brass Tacks Theatre. John is currently at work on a one act play commissioned by Actor's Theatre of Louisville . . . *Steven Dietz's* WANDERLUST, commissioned by Illusion Theatre, will tour the Upper Midwest from Feb. - May, then open in Mpls. for a four week run . . . *Gary Amdahl* has been nominated to attend the Sundance Institute this summer. Gary's MEDICINE LAKE was given a workshop and reading by the Cricket Theatre as part of their Works-in-Progress series . . . *Kevin Kling* performed his one-actor show 21-A for a nearly sold out six-week run in December, and is working on a new one-actor show for himself called AUGUST, about a clown who says bad things about everyone, even mimes . . . *Bill Borden's* THE ONLY WOMAN AWAKE IS THE WOMAN WHO HAS HEARD THE FLUTE will be produced at the University Of North Dakota in March '85 . . . *Marilyn Seven* has been commissioned by The Science Museum of Minnesota to write two scripts for production this spring. Marilyn's POWER PLAYS will be read at American Theatre of Actors in April . . . *Jaime Meyer's* one act play HARRY AND CLAIRE, commissioned by Actor's Theatre of Louisville, was read at the Center in Feb. Jaime is also at work on a commissioned piece for Illusion Theatre, and on a show based on STAGE COMBAT to be produced by Quicksilver Stage next fall. *John Fenn's* play SERVANTS' CHRISTMAS, produced by The Great North American History in December '84, played to 100.4% capacity (four-tenths of the audience sitting on each other's laps?) John is also in rehearsal for DINIZULU'S BEADS, which will play at the Ordway, Chimera and Landmark Center Theatres. And he has been selected as a judge for the Region III FACT Festival (Festival of American Community Theatres) . . . *Martha Boesing* has been invited to attend The Women's Theatre Festival in Boston, as a guest playwright. Martha gave a lecture/performance at the U. of M.'s Coffman Union on "The Lineage Of Our Muses, Public and Private". Her play, ANTIGONE TOO: RITES OF LOVE AND DEFIANCE, will open at DePauw, Indiana in March . . .

Quicksilver Stage's production of "21A" by Kevin Kling, directed by Steven Dietz, played to sold out houses for six weeks. Quicksilver Stage is a theatre for new plays founded by Center playwrights Kling, Dietz, Jaime Meyer and designer Lori Sullivan.

Early in 1986, the newsletter of the Playwrights' Center in Minneapolis noted the success of *21A*, which Kling later performed Off Broadway and around the world.

21A

Cast

RON HUBER
GLADYS
CHAIRMAN FRANCIS
STUDENT
NOT DAVE
CAPTAIN TWELVEPACK
STEVE
JIM SHIPLY

All parts are played by one actor. In addition, CASHIER, CHAIRMAN STEWART, and CUSTOMER are heard as off-stage voices. There are actually two STEVEs: one that the audience can see, and one that the characters on the bus can see. The character STEVE explains this. So it's clear to the reader, the STEVE the audience sees will be typed *STEVE*, and the STEVE the characters see will be typed *Steve*.

SCENE: The play takes place on the 21A bus that runs between Minneapolis and St. Paul. The bus is parked during the action at the beginning of the route. On the bus are a driver's seat, complete with portable cushion, and at least seven other seats for passengers. Also a money box, or till, in the front. Other decorations, such as a steering wheel or overhead ads, are optional.

AT RISE: The <u>LIGHTS</u> fade up on the bus with RON HUBER at the wheel. He is smoking a cigarette and doing a crossword puzzle. There is a five-letter word he can't get. Suddenly he turns to a seat.

RON HUBER: Pardon my French, but screw the Twins, that's how 'bout 'em. *(He goes back to the puzzle for a second.)* What am I, a goldang weatherman? I don't know; it'll clear up. *(Goes back to the puzzle. Suddenly he looks in the rear-view mirror, jumps up, and runs to the back of the bus.)* Hey! Hey! Git away from there, you kids. Git, I say. This ain't no toy. Git, I say. *(He returns to his seat.)*

Dang kids, they play on anything. I get a new gas meter for the house and the next thing I know some neighbor kid is rolling by on the old one. Made a goldang go-kart outta it. Fifty bucks says I can leave something, anything, in my yard and the next day some neighbor kid is selling tickets to it. Oh yeah, you can count on it.

What, this route here? Oh, about two years now. I've driven most of the others, though, your 2, your 3, 4, 7, 12, 17 . . . I even drove the 6 for a while. This 21 is a good route, though. Ain't a day goes by I don't say, "Shit, I never seen that before." It's a different kind of people, see. Poor? I bet there ain't two bucks on this whole bus. Weary? Some of these people have been through stuff a cat wouldn't live through. Crazy? No way. They're just as sane as you or me. Oh, they're a little odd, most of them, you can bet on that. I don't know how they keep from crackin' up.

Me? I go up north fishing with my brother-in-law, that would be Ray. Cripes, we catch the fish, really knock 'em down. Last year we limited out on northern and walleye both. And the beauty of that country . . . Shit. We were sitting there, casting by the shore, and I seen four deer come down for a drink. I says, "Lookee there, Ray, I'd give fifty, no, a hundred bucks for my deer rifle right now." See we got another three months before deer season so I just threw a rock.

You should meet this guy Ray, though. He runs a chicken farm with my sister and two kids, that would be Joe and Bill. But these chickens, you don't eat 'em, see? Ray teaches 'em how to play Tic-Tac-Toe and then sells them to fairs.

Ron Huber.

He makes pretty good money and they're good, too, boy. Shoot, I tried all day, never could beat this one. But at these fairs they're in these little boxes, see? And pretty soon some of them chickens start to crack up. Well lookit, one minute they're a chicken on a farm and the next minute they're in a little box, trying to outwit a human. And when they lose just once *(He makes a raspberry sound with his mouth.)*, you might as well start mashing the potatoes.

Fichu! Fichu! *(He writes on the crossword puzzle.)* It's a woman's triangular scarf.

The way I see it we're all in some kind of box. Sometimes you find your way out, and sometimes you're stuck, like a chicken and then *(Makes the raspberry.)* it don't matter what bus you're on, a 2, 3, 4 . . . 6, even. I gotta theory on people who thrive in boxes but that will cost you a cinnamon triangle and a cup of coffee at the Super America. Hey, what is that crunchy shit in them cinnamon triangles, anyhow? . . . Oh, yeah? *(He stands up and puts out his cigarette.)*

Say, lookit, folks. I'm going down to the Super America for a cup of coffee, but don't worry, we'll start on time. *(He sets down the crossword and picks up his seat cushion.)* Goldang.

(He exits. BLACKOUT.)

(During the blackout TRAFFIC SOUNDS are heard. The next section is a TAPED interlude so the actor has time to change into GLADYS. A CAR rushes by.)

RON HUBER: Cripes, that was close. So like I'm saying you got your two types of people. People who crave the confinement and security that a box offers and people who . . . don't. Now these box people, like I like to call them, they aren't screwed up necessarily. I think Millard Fillmore was a box person and look at him. Now you can always tell a box person, because when they recall the past, their eyes wander up and to the right. Your middle child is usually a box person. Now, I got a theory on middle children, too, but that will run you another cinnamon triangle. Hey. Hey, where are you going? *(FOOTSTEPS are heard running off.)* Ah, to hell with you, then. I'll buy my own cinnamon triangle.

(<u>LIGHTS</u> *up on GLADYS. She has curlers in her hair, tucked under a brightly colored scarf. She wears a long coat and carries two large shopping bags in addition to her purse. She goes right for the seats at the front of the bus marked "Handicapped" and sets a bag of groceries on either side of her—taking up a total of three seats. Pause. She smiles, then turns to the unseen STUDENT.*)

GLADYS: I know why you're staring, honey. I know that look: I know what you're thinking and I don't blame you a bit. I'd think it too, 'cause I don't miss much in this old world, and you're right, this is a lot of food for one cat. But half of it is for my husband. Potpies for Big Bob, little Friskies for Little Bob. I'll grab something later. But you see how looks are deceiving? I'm fifty-eight. What are you? What are you reading? See what I mean?

It's like I'm telling Ruby. She worked at the fair this year where you throw a dart at balloons and this little kid comes up to play, well, he was too little for darts. But Ruby gave him one anyway, and before she could turn around, he'd thrown it and it stuck in her nose. Well, if you knew Ruby, that ain't such an amazing shot, but that dart stuck in her nose, and she pulled it out and gave the kid his money back, which I never would have done, but she told this to the Thursday Forum and all the girls laughed until I told Ruby about lockjaw and how it wasn't a laughing matter and when did she have her last tetanus shot? Well, it had been over three years, and everyone stopped laughing and told Ruby she better go in for a shot. Ruby said "Oh, I'll be all right," but she was awfully quiet for the rest of the night, and I caught her several times wiggling her jaw in the corner. Until the next day she went in for that shot, but I think it was too late. And I told that to Big Bob and he says, "Who cares?" and I said "You should, Big Bob."

See, Big Bob keeps saying he's got cancer, but I think it's gas. But he won't have it checked. And just the other day Mrs. Stitt's dog, Tilly, died and they found a tumor the size of Utah in poor Tilly. But Big Bob oughtta know: he's had two heart attacks. He told me once if he had a million dollars, guess what he'd buy? And I said, "A boat, like Babe Winkelman on that show you're watching," but he said, "Nope, I'd buy my health." Well, I started to tell him how no amount of money can buy health 'cause there's a lot of sick people on the *Love*

Boat—that's my show—and why would they go on a cruise when they could have an operation? Well, I tried to tell Big Bob, but he'd already got back to his show, and no amount of talking can pull him out.

(Swings her purse at someone who has boarded the bus and stumbled onto her— it is CAPTAIN TWELVEPACK, unseen at this point.) Hey, watch where you're stepping, mister. You could've broke my leg. You see my leg there, don't you? How would you like that? Breaking an old lady's leg. You drunks disgust me. Go on! Now get away! Get away! My husband will seek you out and kill you. He'll kill you and I'll watch. He hates disgusting men like you, so it would be no great chore. YOU DAMN DRUNKS MAKE ME SICK.

(back to the STUDENT) Those damn drunks make me sick. I don't have the patience for them, but I used to when I sang. That's right, I was a singer. I almost turned professional, but I didn't. I sang for servicemen, and some of them would get so drunk. But there was a war on, so they had a reason. NOT LIKE SOME PEOPLE I COULD POINT OUT. And that's where I met Big Bob, and the next day he took me to see the movie *Give Out Sisters,* which is still my favorite movie, with the Andrews Sisters, Dan Daily Jr., Grace McDonald, and Charles Butterworth as Professor Woof. And we sat through it twice with my knee sweating on Big Bob's hand. Then we went out for a soda and he said I sang better than the Andrews Sisters and I said "Go on" and he said "Way better" and kissed me right there on the lips in public, which was a big deal for me because I'd never been kissed before except by relatives and my Uncle Ted, but I'd seen movies so I knew just how I would if I ever got the chance. So, I kissed him and asked right away what it was like. That's the only time I've ever seen Big Bob off guard. But finally he said, "Like saxophones and satin." *(Her first pause)* Saxophones and satin, *(pause)* I melted. Romantic language does that to me. I melt.

(CHAIRMAN FRANCIS enters.) What's that? Huh? Oh, no thanks, honey. Don't waste your time with me. I'm saved every Sunday at 9 a.m. on channel 11. But I appreciate the offer. *(CHAIRMAN FRANCIS moves away; GLADYS turns back to the STUDENT.)*

Gladys.

Poor kid. I hope he has another suit. Honestly. I know his plight and it's a tough road. My Uncle Ted used to save people on buses after the accident, but he really was a minister. He married Big Bob and I. I was only seventeen, but I knew Big Bob was for me, so we got married. He'll say he caught me, but don't believe it. It's always up to the woman. And a lot of women were after him, too. Sure they were. See, Big Bob was beautiful. I know you're not supposed to say that about men, but he was. And he'd touch people. Everyone. He'd be talking to you and soon you'd realize he was touching you. And every woman I knew was after that special touch. You bet they were. But I got it. You bet I did.

After the wedding reception we were so nervous—you know how that is—but we went to a hotel and I thought everything went just fine, but in the morning Big Bob was still nervous. I thought it was me, so I laid down and cried. Right there. I found out later it's called "premature ejaculation" and 39 million Americans suffer from it. I also found out they're not the 39 million Americans who are suffering. But I wasn't worried. I figured sooner or later it would go away. And it did.

(Steve appears.) Oh. Shhhh. Shhhh. Don't stare now. Don't stare. Why, hello, Steve. How are you? I am fine, thank you. *(Steve passes by; she returns her attention to the STUDENT.)*

He's retarded. Talks to himself for hours. He thinks that he's talking to another kid, but there's nobody there. Spooky. You know, he can name every city in the world that has a K-Mart. It's amazing. If you're riding the whole route, you should ask him to do it. Makes you want to travel. Go ahead. It's okay and his name is Steve. I think he has one of those special brains like he can memorize K-Marts, but he can't tie his shoes. It's like Big Bob. You name a city, and he'll tell you what football team plays there. Or he'll laugh and say there ain't no team from there. Big Bob ain't retarded though. Go ahead and talk to him. I won't say another word.

(Long silence) We never had any kids, not that we didn't want them. We did have a Vista cruise station wagon with imitation wood paneling and room in back for kids, and a Kenmore washer-dryer, double load, Spegal 60609—but

we were never graced with kids. We made plans even. Big Bob used to say his son would play football and go to college and be better than his old man. I said, "I don't care, just so he never says 'shut up' or watches the *Three Stooges*." Big Bob says, "What's wrong with the *Three Stooges*?" I say, "Too violent." Big Bob says, "The kid's gotta learn sometime." I say, "Wouldn't it be nice if he never did?" Big Bob says, "No kid of mine's gonna be ignorant." I say, "Just pretend." Big Bob says, "Shut up."

(Turns to CAPTAIN TWELVEPACK.) Hey, leave him alone. He's retarded. You damn drunk. I don't care what he threw at you. Leave him alone.

(Back to the STUDENT) Drinking is so important to men. Like the other night, Big Bob's watching *Monday Night Football* and the phone rings. So, I answer it and the man asks, "Is Bob around?" and I know it ain't halftime so I say, "No, can I take a message?" He says, "Tell Bob . . . saxophones and satin." And then he leaves a number. So, I wait till halftime and I tell Big Bob a man called and said, "Saxophones and satin." Big Bob says, "Oh, yeah? I haven't heard that in years." And I'm thinkin' *me neither,* but the sound of it still sends me. So I ask what's it mean. Big Bob says, "Aw, that's army talk, you wouldn't understand." I say, "I bet I would." Big Bob smiles and says, "Saxophones and satin. That's the great feeling of getting real drunk and then laid. *(pause)*

So, after the game, I told Big Bob I wanted a pet. He says, "Why?" "To keep me company," I say. "Okay," says Big Bob, "Don't get a cat. Get a dog. Because a dog is loyal, but a cat don't care about nothing but itself." I say, "I like cats." Big Bob gives me his full attention and says, "If you die and you're locked in your house, a dog will sit there and starve to death—but a cat will eat you. Now, what do you want?" So, I got a cat and named it Little Bob. I feed Big Bob, but I talk to Little Bob. They hate each other. Like the other night I was making Jell-O sal—

(CAPTAIN TWELVEPACK bumps into her.) Look out! I've had enough of you. You don't scare me. You damn drunk. I've lived with your type for thirty-one years. You disgust me. *(pause)* What? How dare you . . . You'd WHAT? . . . Ahh, you'd WHAT? . . . *(smiles)* . . . Really? Then what? Oh, yeah? . . . I am? Oh, no, I

couldn't . . . I really couldn't . . . Oh, no, behind you. That man has a gun! AHH, Steve let him go! No, Bob, look out! AHHHHHHHHHHHH!

(Two GUNSHOTS are heard; stage fades quickly to black.)

(During this blackout NOISES from the inside of a Super America Service Station are heard. The actor is becoming CHAIRMAN FRANCIS in this taped interlude.)

CASHIER: Okay. Go ahead, pump number five is clear. Get any gas?

RON HUBER: No. Thanks, though.

CASHIER: What can I get you?

RON HUBER: I been looking here . . . I don't see any of them cinnamon triangles.

CASHIER: These are them, right here. How many do you want?

RON HUBER: Those are round though.

CASHIER: We changed the shape. How many?

RON HUBER: They're the same as the other ones?

CASHIER: Yeah, only round.

RON HUBER: They don't look the same.

CASHIER: Well, they are. How many do you want?

RON HUBER: I know, they don't have that crunchy shit on them.

CASHIER: We stopped putting that on.

RON HUBER: Oh. How come?

CASHIER: Regulations.

RON HUBER: Oh, yeah? Huh.

CASHIER: I can sprinkle some on if you'd like.

RON HUBER: No, that's okay. I finally found out what it was. How come they crunch?

CASHIER: They're toasted. How many?

RON HUBER: Uh . . . Two. No, them two right there. Yeah.

(LIGHTS up: GLADYS's groceries remain where they were, in addition to her purse, which sits on her chair. The lights reveal CHAIRMAN FRANCIS. He wears a dark, ill-fitting suit and speaks with a Boston accent. He approaches GLADYS, tentatively.)

CHAIRMAN FRANCIS: Good morning. Are you pleased with the status quo? Is your faith serving you well? *(pause)* I see. Thank you. *(He approaches CAPTAIN TWELVEPACK.)* Good morning. Are you pleased with the status quo? Is your faith serving you—uh, who, me? Unh-unh, unh-unh, unh-unh. I see. Thank you.

(He approaches the last seat on the bus—where JIM SHIPLY will sit when we see him. CHAIRMAN FRANCIS sits in a seat facing this one and speaks to JIM.) Do you mind if I sit here? Thank you. Are you pleased with the status quo, is your faith serving you well, do you have a hard time sleeping at night, is the future unclear and do you feel helpless as to its outcome? Of course you do. Could I ask a minute of your time? It could perhaps give you peace of mind. Thank you. You have heard of the faith of Democratic Progression? Uh, no. Well, I am Chairman Francis, and the man out there pursuing the driver of this vehicle is Chairman Stewart, and we are here from Boston as part of our two-year term as missionaries to that particular faith. And what is your name? I see. Then perhaps we may simply call you "Mister Chairman."

(To the entire bus:) All in favor? *(Raises his hand.)* Aye. Opposed? *(Pause. Back to JIM:)* Very well. Motion carried. Let it come to pass. *(A podium springs out from CHAIRMAN FRANCIS's shirt.)* Mr. Chairman, as I speak to you, I see an all-too-familiar look on your face. A look as if to say, "Before me stands a happy man. A man who is ready, come what may. I wonder how that man achieved this inner peace." Now, Mr. Chairman, you seem like an intelligent man. A man who cares about the world around him. A man who witnesses injustice and evil and is disgusted, but has no recourse. Mr. Chairman, if this disgust remains unchecked, it will build up and up with no outlet, no escape, festering and swelling like a giant ball, a ball of pus with no relief, Mr. Chairman, no relief. Well, this is your lucky day, Mr. Chairman, for I am here to relieve you.

"How?" you may ask. Because Mr. Chairman, the church of Democratic Progression believes in change. Mr. Chairman, evil, evil, that dirty little filthy guy, evil is constantly changing, while the church has remained firm and happy sitting on its foundation. Evil loves that, Mr. Chairman. Evil thinks that is a real hoot. Because evil can chip away at that foundation. Evil has its work clearly cut out for it, while the church must stand there and take it. Well, not anymore, Mr. Chairman. Change is what we're all about. Our church is the street, our faith is the people, and our laws are constantly changing. If a law offends us, we pluck it out. If a minister offends us, we pluck him out and elect a new minister who is young and strong and can recognize evil's ever-changing face.

We don't believe in miracles; we believe in action. But action takes money. Mr. Chairman, the church of Democratic Progression needs your financial support. Now, Mr. Chairman, how much would you pay to nip evil in the bud? Now I'm not talking about wiping out evil entirely, just your own little personal dark speck. Would you pay forty dollars, Mr. Chairman? Thirty dollars? Twenty dollars, the price of four filthy movies? NO. Mr. Chairman, for just fifteen dollars a month you can keep a chairman, like myself, on the streets fighting evil on your behalf. What do you say, Mr. Chairman, only fifteen dollars! I see. Then perhaps you would like to purchase a copy of *Our Progress* for only five dollars. I see. Then perhaps you would like to make a tax-deductible donation for the incumbent minister. I see. Then perhaps you would like to

Chairman Francis.

be the incumbent minister. I see. Then perhaps you would care to leave your name and address and another chairman, such as Chairman Stewart, could call on you at a more convenient time. I see. Well, I'm sorry I've wasted your time. I will now leave you to sit in your inner torment.

(He moves to the front of the bus and tears off his podium, setting it on the chair in front of where NOT DAVE will sit.) Mr. Chairman, I would greatly appreciate it if you would wipe that smirk off your face. Perhaps you think of me as strange or lost. Well, I assure you I am not. It's not like I'm following some baldheaded guru who wants to take me camping for the rest of my life. No. Certain unknowns have been revealed to me. See for yourself, Mr. Chairman. Look outside. Look at the wickedness and the violence. Or read the paper, read the paper, Mr. Chairman. I read that paper every day, and it frightens me. And I see my father safe and content in his Easy-Boy recliner lusting after Haley Mills, eating his huge red meat Dagwood Bumstead sandwiches and changing slower than Blondie's girlish figure and IT SICKENS ME. Well, you can sit there too, Mr. Chairman, you can sit there on your fat foundation. Or you can rise up. You can ride that crest, you can say ENOUGH—That's it, Mr. Chairman, rise up, that's it, Mr. Chairman, reach in that pocket, that's right, Mr. Chairman, dig deep, that's it, that's . . .

I move we all recognize the man with the large handgun. All in favor, aye. All opposed. Motion carried. Let it come to pass.

(He dives behind a seat as the <u>LIGHTS</u> go down and we hear two <u>GUNSHOTS</u>.)

(In this blackout the <u>NOISES</u> continue from the same Super America. The actor is becoming the STUDENT. Again, this is taped.)

CASHIER: Okay. Will that be all?

RON HUBER: No, I'll be getting some coffee, but first I need the key to the restroom.

CASHIER: I'm afraid it's already out.

RON HUBER: Well, there ain't nobody out there. I already knocked.

CASHIER: Brother, somebody must've walked off with the key.

RON HUBER: What'll I do? I gotta go.

CASHIER: Here, use this screwdriver. It works just as good.

RON HUBER: Okay. How do I do it?

CASHIER: Push the door in as hard as you can.

RON HUBER: Yeah.

CASHIER: Push the screwdriver next to the bolt.

RON HUBER: Okay.

CASHIER: Okay. Then with your other hand, jiggle the knob.

RON HUBER: Yeah.

CASHIER: Now, shake the screwdriver in between the latch and the bolt. There's just barely enough room, but it fits.

RON HUBER: So now both hands are jiggling.

CASHIER: Uh huh. Then, when you have the screwdriver wedged, just twist it and the door opens.

RON HUBER: That don't sound too hard.

CASHIER: No. And if you can't get in I'll give you the key to the women's.

RON HUBER: I'll get in.

CASHIER: And don't forget to lock it when you're done.

(LIGHTS up; CHAIRMAN FRANCIS's book is sitting on the chair he last sat in. The lights now reveal the STUDENT. He wears a university sweatshirt and holds a few large books. He reads for a few moments, then looks up at GLADYS.)

STUDENT: I'm a student. *(Pause.)* Political Science. *(Two GUNSHOTS are heard as LIGHTS go quickly to black.)*

(This blackout is also in the Super America. The actor is changing into NOT DAVE.)

RON HUBER: Hey, lady, over here. Over here. Hey, lady, I'm back.

CASHIER: Any problems?

RON HUBER: No. I got a garage door like that at home. Here's your screwdriver back, and the key. It was on the sink.

CASHIER: Thanks. They always leave the key.

RON HUBER: Yeah. Hey, how 'bout that coffee?

CASHIER: Help yourself.

RON HUBER: What are these plastic mugs here?

CASHIER: What? Oh . . . If you buy coffee in one you can keep the cup.

RON HUBER: Big deal. It costs twice as much as coffee in a Styrofoam one.

CASHIER: Yeah, well, you pay sixty-nine cents for the first cup and every time you come in you can get a refill for a dime.

RON HUBER: Christ, I'll save a fortune.

CASHIER: And they don't tip over.

The Student.

(LIGHTS up. The STUDENT's book remains on his chair. Lights reveal NOT DAVE, sitting in a comfortable corduroy coat and a hat. He holds an Esquire *magazine. He sits looking out the window. Just then he suddenly looks to the front of the bus.)*

NOT DAVE: My name isn't Dave. I'm not Dave. *(addressing the seat next to him now:)* No, I'm not. No. No. No. No. No. No. No. No. No. No. No. No. *(pause)* No. No. *(pause)* Jim. Bob. Ed. Bill. Roger. Fred. Sam. Mike. Pete. Herman. Jim. Dave *(Grimaces. Pause).* Abdul. Vito. Horatio. Thucydides. *(Suddenly ducks and then looks to back of bus.)* HEY, LOOK OUT. *(to chair next to him:)* No. No. No. Look, I'm sick of this. Leave me alone. LEAVE ME ALONE!

(BLACKOUT. Two GUNSHOTS.*)*

(Another blackout in the Super America. The actor is becoming CAPTAIN TWELVEPACK.)

CHAIRMAN STEWART: Uh. Sir. Sir. Are you pleased with the status quo and is your faith serving you well?

RON HUBER: Yeah. What the hell is this?

CHAIRMAN STEWART: My name is Chairman Stewart and with my partner, Chairman Francis, we are serving as missionaries for the faith of Democratic Progression. Could I ask a minute of your time?

RON HUBER: No.

CHAIRMAN STEWART: Well, then, perhaps you could leave your name and address and we could contact you at a more convenient time.

RON HUBER: No.

CHAIRMAN STEWART: I see. Thank you very much.

RON HUBER: Hey. Hey, wait, kid. How much area do you and your buddy cover?

Not Dave.

CHAIRMAN STEWART: Well, our parish is quite small. Chairman Francis and I must cover the entire five-state area.

RON HUBER: So, do you ever get up north?

CHAIRMAN STEWART: Yes. As a matter of fact, we will be in the northern sector around August.

RON HUBER: No shit.

CHAIRMAN STEWART: Yes, around August.

RON HUBER: Here, I'll give you the name of a guy who would love to talk to you guys. When you get to Brainerd call this number, and ask for Ray.

CHAIRMAN STEWART: Ray.

RON HUBER: Yeah, Ray. Oh, Ray is gonna shit. Tell him Ron Huber sent you, and don't take no for an answer.

CHAIRMAN STEWART: Yes, yes. Thank you, Chairman Ron. I will be sure to include you in my next speech.

RON HUBER: That's okay. Glad I could help . . . Ray is gonna shit.

(NOT DAVE's hat and magazine remain on his seat. CAPTAIN TWELVEPACK's voice is heard from off.)

CAPTAIN TWELVEPACK: The siege has ended! Storm the gate! *(CAPTAIN TWELVEPACK enters, trips on the bus steps, and crashes into the money till: He wears a tattered old executive's coat and an empty twelve-pack box on his head which covers all but his mouth and one ear, which pokes out of the side of the cardboard.)* DA-DA-DA! Yield or die at the hand of Captain Twelvepack! *(Pulls himself to his feet.)* I'll take that as a yield. *(Steps on GLADYS's feet.)* Out of my way, baseborn slut. Blah blah blah. Bring on this hapless husband. I'll soil his tunic with his own blood.

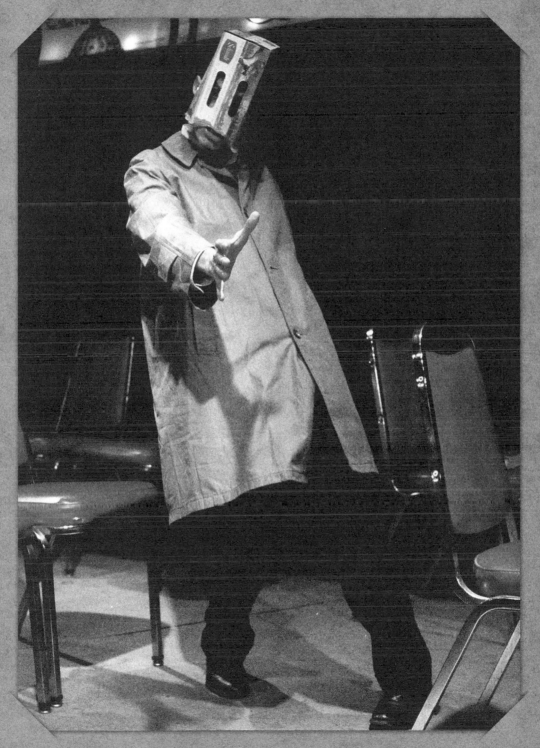

Captain Twelvepack.

(Looks to the back of the bus.) DAVE *(walks to and sits next to NOT DAVE).* Dave, over here. Dave, it's me. God, it's good to see you, Dave, you bastard. How've you been, Dave, ol' pal? *(pause)* You are too Dave. Yes, you are. Yes, you are. Yes. Yes. Yes. Yes. Yes. Yes. Yes. Yes. Yes. Yes. GODDAMN IT, DAVE, YOU ARE TOO.

(Cries.) I'm sorry, Dave. I didn't mean it. Now, come on. Guess who I am in here. Come on, guess. Guess. GUESS. *(pause)* No. No. No. No. No. No. No. No. No. No. *(laughs)* You're Dave. No. No. NO. NO. Here, I'll give you a hint. *(whispers)* Phil. That's right: it's me all the time. You don't remember me, do you, Dave? Hey, Dave, remember the time you stole my wife? I never killed you for that, did I, Dave? So, how've you been?

(Turns to CHAIRMAN FRANCIS, who stands above him.) Keep your distance, friar. I have no need of your Saxon god. Now, back off or I'll send you to him in a box.

(Turns back to NOT DAVE:) Dave! Yeah, Phil. Right. I'll tell you, Dave, two weeks ago I had a beautiful job, a full-time wife—my wife, how could you do that, Dave? You were my best friend. *(Drops his head.)* I know. I know I deserved it. I know. I know. I know. *(Voice becomes almost inaudibly soft.)* I know. Hey, Dave. If I fall asleep while I'm telling you this, wake me up, okay? Or they put me in jail. JAIL, DAVE.

(Sits up, confidential to NOT DAVE:) I'm on my way to rendezvous with a man named Fat Max. He's laying siege on a cigarette machine on Seventh. The rest of the troops are back at the bridge where I live. I LIVE UNDER A GODDAMN BRIDGE, DAVE. FREE AS THE WIND. I'M A CONCRETE CRUSADER, THAT'S WHAT. The other guys named me Captain Twelvepack and made me this helmet. How do you like it? I could probably make you one, Dave, yeah, no problem

(Turns suddenly to back of bus.) HEY, WATCH WHERE YOU'RE THROWING THAT APPLE, YOU GODDAMNED MINION! *(To GLADYS:)* I DON'T CARE IF HE IS RETARDED: HE ALMOST KILLED MY BEST FRIEND! *(back to NOT DAVE:)* Goddammit, Dave, I'm not meant for this street life. I should be out in the suburbs, for cryin' out loud, in a ranch-style home with a basketball hoop and a sprinkler

and a dog with a name. I'm like in a panic, and these other guys can sense it. They pretend they're real nice, but they smoke all my cigarettes and make me wear this fricken' hat and I know they're goin' through my stuff right now. I know they sent me to meet Fat Max so they could go through my stuff, but what am I supposed to say? "No, you guys, 'cause you're gonna go through my stuff?"—THEY'D LOVE THAT. They'd pretend I hurt their feelings and then, boy, would I get it.

I mean, these guys are hard, Dave. One guy called Special Ed—he sleeps on broken glass. And not a scratch. And Tom Cat has part of his cheekbone exposed from an accident—and they use it as the company bottle opener, Dave. But these guys are small potatoes compared to "the Dog." That's what they call him: "the Dog." This is one weird effin' guy, Dave. It's the first night I'm there under this bridge, and I ask if it's okay that I stay. They say, "It's okay with us, but you've got to ask the Dog." "Okay," I say, "who's the Dog?" And they point to this hairy guy who's crouched down by part of the trestle.

So, I walk over and say, "Are you the Dog?" And he looks at me and smiles and there's just two teeth left in his head—and even they're goners, Dave—and he says, "Yes. Please have a seat." So I do. I mean, here's this grimy, hairy vagabond with the manners of a butler. So I ask the Dog if I can stay with them, and he says, "Of course. Of course. If you can manage the responsibility." I say, "WHAT?" He says, "See that skyline? Someday that will all be yours." I say, "WHAT?" "I hope you're ready, because sooner or later we own every building in this city. It's part of our inheritance. As survivors of mankind's ingenuity we are heirs, and someday, son, this will all be yours. The older it gets, the closer we get. *(He is now standing above NOT DAVE.)*

Just wait for it to die. Just wait right here where the twelve pack is captain and the bottle is king. Wait right here with the rubbish and the scavengers. Wait right here with the roaches and the dogs, the roaches and the dogs, ROACHES AND DOGS, ROACHES AND DOGS AND DOGS AND DOGS DOGS DOGS DOGS DOGS DOGS! *(Howls like a mad dog; stops abruptly.)* And then he dropped down and scratched his ear with his foot, Dave. He took this empty twelve pack and he jammed it on my head and said "I christen you CAPTAIN TWELVEPACK. Remove this and forfeit your inheritance." And then we drank and drank and drank and I snuck away and coiled myself as tight as I could under that bridge and tried to be invisible and hoped some deranged SOB didn't kill me while I was still awake.

(Silence; he slowly sits back down.) I can't be like them, Dave. I look at these guys and they know they could be me and have money and teeth. And I look at them and I know that no amount of hardship could give me that soul. I can't have that soul. Shit. *(pause)* Hey, I'm making you sweat. You're not doing that just to cheer me up, are you, Dave? You're all right, Dave. Care for a smoke? *(Checks his coat very briefly.)* Oh, I'm all out—you got one? Well, how about you give me change, and I'll go get some? Well, how 'bout giving me a buck; I'll get change? Well, how 'bout *loanin'* me a buck? Hey, there's no reason to get uppity, Dave. Conversation is free. Shit, sorry. I'm alive and now I must depart. *(Stands.)* Keep your sword sharp and your senses dull. And say "Hi" to my wife for me, Dave. I'd tip my hat, but as heir to the city, it would not be wise.

(He moves down the aisle and stumbles again onto GLADYS.) One side, sultry wench, I said, one side. I ought to ravage you on the spot. Have my way with you. *(pause)* Good lord . . . how could I be so blind? Your beauty overwhelms me. I am drawn to you like a magnet *(which he is)*. Come away with me and be my queen. Come on. Yes, you can. Yes, you can. Yes. Yes. *(pause)* What? A gun? *(Turns to face back of bus)* Behind me, fair maid. Bullets cannot harm me. Leave this Saxon dog to me. Hold him steady, stable boy. I'll speed his soul to hell! DA-DA-DA!!! *(He charges the back of the bus as the <u>LIGHTS</u> go to black. <u>GUNSHOTS</u> are heard.)* Dave, I am slain.

(<u>BLACKOUT</u> at the Super America. The actor is changing into STEVE.)

CASHIER: May I help you?

CUSTOMER: Yeah, I want a brownie.

RON HUBER: Hey, what's this doing here?

CUSTOMER: Are these things fresh?

CASHIER: We get them fresh every day from Mrs. Moms.

RON HUBER: Lady. What's this doing here?

CASHIER: What? That's cream.

RON HUBER: Yeah, well where's the Coffee Mate?

CASHIER: We ran out so we had to use real cream.

RON HUBER: Christ. First the cinnamon triangles and now this. This place is going to hell. What? What, am I supposed to put that liquid shit in perfectly good coffee?

CASHIER: Look, cream is better than powder. It's more healthy for you.

RON HUBER: You think I come to SA for my health. Now you march to the back and get me some Coffee Mate, young lady. I got a bus waiting.

CASHIER: I told you: we're all out.

RON HUBER: Well, I can't drink it black.

CASHIER: Look, we sell Coffee Mate. You can buy a jar of it in aisle three if you want it that bad.

RON HUBER: What, you want me to buy five gallons of the shit when all I need is four tablespoons? Where's the manager of this place?

CASHIER: I told you we're all out.

RON HUBER: Then find some. I come to SA because I know I won't be surprised like this. I got faith in SA, and once one goes *(Makes the raspberry sound.)* the whole franchise is shot, as far as I'm concerned. So you find my Coffee Mate or lose a regular customer.

CASHIER: I'll look in the back.

RON HUBER: Good.

(LIGHTS up. CAPTAIN TWELVEPACK's helmet remains on his chair. STEVE enters very slowly, walking with extra care and breathing loudly. He gets to GLADYS and pauses for a moment.)

STEVE: Hi, Gladys. *(He continues toward the back of the bus. He reaches his seat and sits.)* Steve told me to stay here and don't move an inch. *(He looks to the seat right next to him, where "Steve" sits. Then he moves one inch.)* There. What do you think of that, Steve? Oh, come on, you big baby. I told you I was sorry. Come on, Steve, talk to me.

(To audience:) Steve and I aren't talking now 'cause I made him mad. Real mad. We were at the doctor's and got in a big fight. A real big fight and now things look bad for us. Especially Steve. He enjoys his freedom and now it's in jeopardy. We might have to live in confinement for awhile and Steve blames me. So we aren't talking.

(To Steve:) Steve Steve Steve Steve Steve.

(To audience:) Nope . . . clammed up. I don't mind. I make friends easily. It's a gift. But Steve holds a grudge. It's his own fault, though. See, Steve is really smart and can look at something and never forget what it looks like. Ever. He can tell you how to build a Piper Cub 'cause he saw the plans once. Or he can tell you the highest elevation of every continent. But he thinks he's really cool 'cause he can name all the cities in the world that have a K-Mart. In alphabetical order.

(To Steve:) Well, who can't, Steve?

Steve.

(To audience:) So, this morning we were at the doctor's office and Steve wanted to show how smart he was 'cause he knows they're thinking about locking us up. So, he starts going through the K-Marts beginning with "A." Well, I read this morning in the paper they're opening a new K-Mart in Burnsville. I'm sitting there nice and quiet and polite the whole time he and the doctor are talking, and then Steve starts reciting and gets to the "B's" and oops—he missed Burnsville. So, I calmly say, "Burnsville." 'Cause I didn't want Steve to look bad in front of the doctor. I was only trying to help, and Steve said, "What?" And I said, "Burnsville, Steve." And he said, "What about it?" And I said, "There's a K-Mart in Burnsville." Steve goes "Huh uh" and I go "Uh huh" and Steve goes "Huh uh" and I go "Uh huh, I just read it in the paper today."

And then Steve really lost his cool and yelled at me to shut up or else. And I go, "I was just trying to help, Steve." And Steve goes, "That kind of help is gonna get us put away." And then we really had a plate smasher. *(pause)* The doctor looked confused at first, but then he called a big dude in white and he broke it up.

(To Steve:) That is too how it went. Uh huh. Uh huh. Uh huh. You did too miss Burnsville. You got problems, pal. *(pause, angry)* Take that back, Steve. Take it back or else. *(Watching Steve's movements.)* What are you doing now, Steve? Are you going to eat your lunch? No? You're going to eat that apple? No? You're going to throw that apple? At me? *(Stands and laughs, moving toward NOT DAVE.)* Oh, Steve, I am shaking in my boots. You better not throw that, Steve: you might hurt your wimpy little arm. C'mon, Steve, you couldn't hit the broadside of a K-Mart! *(Sidesteps the toss and laughs, returning to his seat.)* Ha-ha. Missed me by a mile. Oh, now we're not talking again. See, Steve's good around other people—but I can really tick him off.

(To Steve:) So . . . they're sending us away. I wonder where we'll go. St. Peter, maybe. St. Cloud, maybe. Alexandria, maybe. Stillwater, maybe. Shakopee, maybe. Sandstone, maybe. Burnsville, maybe—God, I hope not. I don't know, but after that last outbreak we're going somewhere.

(To audience:) See, people think Steve has an invisible friend. But I'm not,

really. So, when Steve has a big fight with me, all they see is Steve going bonkers. They're afraid he'll hurt himself. They've got good reason, 'cause he's tried before. He tried to kill himself when he was little. See, Steve has always been uncoordinated—sorry, Steve, but it's true—and the other kids would torment him. Well, who could blame 'em? So, when it came time to swim, Steve wouldn't go in the water, 'cause he knew he'd sink and everyone would laugh. So, the teacher tossed him in. Steve could've stood up easy, but instead he let out all his air and went to the bottom and pretended to pour a cup of tea and drink it. Then he put down the cup and layed down. Right there in the pool. They finally pulled him out, but he was in a coma and stayed that way for days. When he came to, I was there. And I've been with him ever since.

See, I won't let him hurt himself. People don't know I help him. They always want to break us up. Even Gladys tried. She's the lady up there with all the cat food. She tried to tell Steve I wasn't here. She tried and tried and tried. Gladys would go "Okay, Steve, you're by yourself now. It's just you and me, honey." And I'd be sitting right there! And I couldn't help but laugh, and when I laugh Steve always laughs.

(To Steve:) Right, Steve?

(To audience:) Still ticked. One time Gladys goes, "Okay, Steve, close your eyes." And he did. And then she goes, "Now when you open them, your friend will be gone." Steve said, "No, he won't." But while his eyes were closed I snuck up and hid behind another seat on the bus, and when he opened them, I was gone. And boy did he scream bloody murder. And then I jumped up and said "Steve," and we laughed and laughed and—

(To Steve:) Oh, you smiled, Steve. UH HUH. UH HUH. UH HUH. You're such a liar. *(Reaches in pocket.)* I didn't want to have to do this, Steve. Oh no. Not that. Anything but that. Please, no. *(He pulls out a standard-sized rubber band from his pocket and stretches it around his head at forehead level. As he opens his mouth and eyes wide, the rubber band creeps toward the crown of his head, taking all his hair with it—finally jerking all the hair up into an instant ponytail. He accompanies this with a slowly building scream that crescendos at the proper moment.*

Then, he turns back to Steve for his reaction.) OH, YOU SMILED. YES, YOU DID. UH HUH. UH HUH. UH HUH. UH HUH. You got problems, pal.

(To audience:) Now, when we get sent away, they're going to tell Steve I'm not here, maybe. Or they'll make Steve hate me, maybe. Or they'll drug him so he can't see me, maybe. That's okay—we fight a lot these days, anyhow. If they do send me away, Steve, you'll have to behave. I won't be there to talk you out of being stupid. I'm not worried. Stick to things you know. Like Piper Cubs. Okay? I'll miss you, Steve. *(Follows Steve's movements with his eyes.)* Steve—don't do that. Let him go! Steve. Let him go! SSSSSSSSSSTTTTTTTTTTTEEEEEEEEVVVEEEEEEEEE!

(BLACKOUT. Two GUNSHOTS.)

(The last blackout at the Super America. The actor changes into JIM SHIPLY.)

CASHIER: Here we go. I found two packets, but that's it.

RON HUBER: Thanks. Look, I'm sorry I made such a ruckus over the Coffee Mate.

CASHIER: It's okay. I understand.

RON HUBER: It's just when your body gets used to something, you don't like to throw it out of whack.

CASHIER: Yeah, I know. I'm the same way with Hot Tamales at a movie.

RON HUBER: Oh, yeah?

CASHIER: Yeah. I don't care how good the show is or who I'm with, if I don't have Hot Tamales, I fidget.

RON HUBER: Yeah. I've heard of that.

CASHIER: I can't explain it.

RON HUBER: No sense trying.

CASHIER: But it limits me.

RON HUBER: Yeah, yeah, it does that . . .

CASHIER: And you like to think you can do anything.

RON HUBER: Yeah. Hey, look, I gotta get out of here.

CASHIER: But then you realize you're only human. Excuse me.

Clear on number three.

Where were we?

RON HUBER: Hey, look, I gotta run.

CASHIER: Okay, is that it?

RON HUBER: Yeah. That'll do it.

CASHIER: It comes to a dollar thirty-seven.

RON HUBER: Thanks again. I'll be seeing you.

CASHIER: Have a nice day.

RON HUBER: Yeah, you too.

(*Two* GUNSHOTS *are heard.* LIGHTS *come up on JIM SHIPLY. He has a gun and it's pointed at the seat STEVE was in—the STEVE the audience saw. There are two bullet holes in the seat. The rubber band sits on the seat also. JIM SHIPLY is very nervous.*)

JIM SHIPLY: Ah! Look what you made me do, kid. *(He points the gun at the Steve who tried to grab him.)* Sit down. SIT DOWN. *(JIM follows Steve to his seat with the gun.)* Okay, thanks. Now it's my turn. Nobody move. Nobody panic. *(He suddenly whirls the gun on the STUDENT.)* WHAT! What do you want? . . . Well, you don't have to raise your hand, kid. Just speak . . . Him? *(He points to CAPTAIN TWELVEPACK.)* He can't be dead; I shot over here. *(He points to bullet holes.)* Look, he's breathing, see? *(Points back to TWELVEPACK.)* See that? He's passed out. He's a drunk and he's passed out, that's all. *(Points at the Steve he can see.)* You, kid, calm down. *(Levels the gun on Steve.)* I said, calm down. Thanks.

Okay, look everybody, nobody is dead yet. But now I'm nervous. That's just something we're going to have to deal with. This is not a robbery. I repeat: this is not a robbery. But I'm going to need all your money. So, starting with the lady in the front, take out all your money and hand it to the person behind you until it all gets back to me. Go. *(During this JIM SHIPLY moves the gunpoint from one character to another. After the STUDENT, he continues to point at NOT DAVE and then Steve, then looks in Steve's hand and says:)*

A dollar seven cents? That's it? That's all the money on this bus? Okay. Now I'm mad. That's something else we have to deal with. Somebody is holding out. People must die. First, the kid. *(Points the gun at Steve and then whirls it on the STUDENT.)* WHAT! I told you, you don't have to raise your hand. Well, what is it? . . . Yeah. I was going to do that. *(Points at NOT DAVE.)* You. Dave. Reach in his pockets. *(Points to CAPTAIN TWELVEPACK.)* He called you Dave. Why would he call you Dave if that's not your name? Look, I've got the gun, your name is Dave, reach in his pockets. *(JIM SHIPLY stands and goes to CAPTAIN TWELVEPACK. He watches NOT DAVE reach in the pocket.)* Yuck. What the hell is that? No. No, I've seen enough, put it back.

(Goes to the STUDENT.) Okay. What about you? Wait a minute, are you a student? Oh. *(He turns away.)* Forget it then. *(He goes to CHAIRMAN FRANCIS.)* You—let's have the collection plate. Nothing? All day? You should have hit a number 6. *(He goes to GLADYS.)* That leaves you, lady. All of it on potpies and cat food? All right. I tried. A dollar seven cents, that's it. I tried.

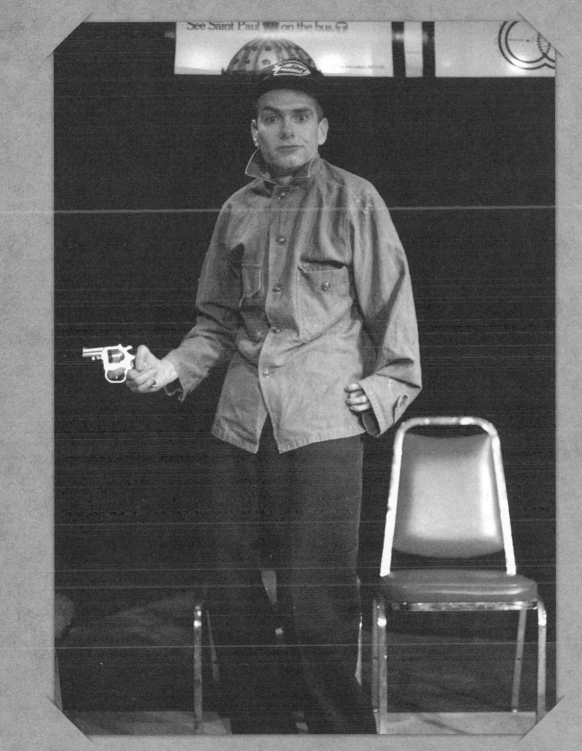

Jim Shiply.

Kid. Come here. *(He points the gun at Steve and keeps it trained on him until Steve is right next to the barrel.)* Put the money in the till, and sit down. *(JIM SHIPLY follows Steve to the till. The SOUND OF MONEY running through a bus till is heard. JIM watches Steve go back to his seat, then turns to the till.)* There you go. Drink it down. Nice and easy. There you go. You'll be alright now. *(SOUND OUT. He puts the gun in his pocket and suddenly turns around.)* That's where your money goes! I watched each one of you get on the bus and forget the till. It's leeches like you that sit in your climate-controlled environment and refuse to feed the bus. And when you starve the bus you strangle the flow and it kills the system! Why don't you litter, for God's sake? Why don't you eat or drink or smoke? Why don't you parade around with electronic devices while you're at it? Or interfere with the operator? Huh? We can abuse the system, right? It won't die. We can afford to lose a route. Sure. We could even lose this route, right? We'd still have a hundred and twenty-two routes left. So big deal. And even if we lost a few more, who cares? So we lose our Saturday service to Rosedale and we drop from second in the nation, behind LA, to eighth . . . behind St. Louis. So what, right? And so we lose convenience fares or Project Mobility. Who cares about the handicapped? And seniors—they can pay full fare just like the rest of us. Well, not on my bus. Not while I'm aboard. Not while I'm alive . . . And have a gun.

Okay. Look. Say it's cold out . . . Twenty below. And dark . . . midnight. And I'm lost in a strange part of town. But I have seventy-five cents. Seventy-five cents. *(Goes to GLADYS.)* Seventy-five cents will get me home to the ones I love. *(To CHAIRMAN FRANCIS:)* Seventy-five cents buys me a captive audience. *(To the STUDENT:)* Gets me an education, *(To CAPTAIN TWELVEPACK:)* a place to sleep, *(To NOT DAVE:)* buys me friends when I need them, *(To Steve:)* and gets rid of them when I don't. And my seventy-five cents insures me that next bus will be there when I need it. And if I don't have correct change . . . I buy a comb. *(He pulls out a handful of combs.)*

I will not bother the driver. The driver . . . If you people had your way this would just be another man out of a job, right? Another man who worked while you slept. A man who was responsible for every action on this bus. The man is a god. Revere him. And take care of your system, or it will die. I've got to go now: I'm due on a 17. And maybe the next time you get on this bus, I won't be here . . . (*Drops hat, <u>BLACKOUT</u>. The following lines are done live in the darkness as the actor moves from the back of the bus to the front. JIM's cap ends up on his chair.*) . . . But maybe I will.

STEVE: Steve. Steve. Over here. He missed me by a mile. Steve, talk to me. Oh, now you're ignoring me. Come on, Steve.

CAPTAIN TWELVEPACK: Dave. Dave.

NOT DAVE: What?

CAPTAIN TWELVEPACK: I knew you were Dave.

STUDENT: Pardon me, sir, before you leave, I have a question.

CHAIRMAN FRANCIS: And it came to pass that Prophet Francis was not assassinated and went on to become minister of local bus service.

GLADYS: You robbers make me sick. Those robbers make me sick. Did you see that bullet? It missed me by an inch. I can't wait to tell Little Bob. (*<u>LIGHTS</u> come up as RON HUBER enters.*)

RON HUBER: Whoa . . . look at that guy. Start mashing the potatoes. Sorry I'm late, folks. They ran out of Coffee Mate at the SA. Can you believe that? Anything happen while I was out? Everybody get their money in the till? Alright. (*He sits in the driver's seat and calls out the first stop.*) Lake Street.

(*The <u>LIGHTS</u> fade to black.*)

End of Play

THE TRUMPET

FROM A MEMORIAL FOR ETHAN JOHNSON OF THE BRASS MESSENGERS

When a trumpet comes out of its case,
ambivalence leaves the room.

The trumpet is a trickster.

The trumpet feels every solo was meant for it.
The trumpet is bad with secrets.
The trumpet doesn't suffer rests well.
Sometimes a trumpet player has a look like, "It wasn't me."

The trumpet loves to wake people up
And to tell them they have to go to bed,
Even though a trumpet never wants to go to bed.

A trumpet loves to say, "They're over there."
And, "We're over here."
And, "We're bigger than you think."
And, "We're bigger than we think."

The trumpet yells "charge"—
Sometimes at the wrong moment.

There are no small mistakes with a trumpet.

A trumpet can't help itself.
A trumpet will always, always, say what it means.

Babies don't fall asleep to trumpets.
The baby that does is one to watch—
And, later in life, give a trumpet.

A trumpet needs compassion.

A trumpet also gushes praise,
Promises a brighter world.
Trumpets knock down walls,
Announce kings and queens.
Trumpets open gates.

And a trumpet can be loyal, sexy, smoky, playful, it brings the party.
The trumpet likes it with the lights on.

Sometimes a trumpet player looks like, "That *was* me."

Even when mournful, a trumpet suppresses a laugh.

Trumpets cut the fog
First and furthest and fearless
From the known to the unknown to the unknowable.

Trumpets don't care how high heaven is,
If anything can get there, it's a trumpet.

And when it does,
A trumpet isn't mistaken for anything else,
It's a trumpet.

PAINTING THE HOUSE

FROM *BACK HOME*

I grew up in a ranch-style rambler, just like the ranch-style rambler next to ours, like the one next to theirs, like the one next to theirs, lined up as far as the eye could see: fifties, pre-fab, suburban, a second home after the starter home from being home from the war. When we flew over our neighborhood in one of my dad's planes, the houses looked like dominoes as far as my peripheral vision would allow. Topple one and the whole neighborhood would collapse.

Our home was just a little different. Our home had a breezeway, a screened-in porch that connected the house to the garage. My brother and I could easily climb that breezeway to the roof of the house to "see what was going on in the neighborhood."

Also, our home was a bit more disheveled than the other homes. My dad never worked on that house. He'd say, "It's a rental, boys, and you never work on a rental."

Paint was chipping off the siding, shingles curled, the broken eaves became housing for birds, critters, and wasps, but my dad held firm. Most of our neighbors tended their homes with loving care, care that seemed to suggest an inner order, that this was how their children were treated, their jobs were going, and their marriages were faring. Their lawns, thick and healthy, lavished with heapin' helpin's of fertilizers and watered with sprinkler systems designed by those who put a man in space. But they owned these homes, fought a war for them. And when a man puts that kind of time and effort into his castle, trespassing is often met with verbal volleys threatening mutilation, obscenities, souls sent hellhound, suggested canine lineage all for cutting across portions of precious sod.

My dad encouraged children to play in the yard. He had his reasons: it packed down the grass. When the neighbors called to complain about the length of the lawn, my dad agreed things were getting a bit out of hand. So to speed up the process, Dad bought a tetherball kit, cemented a coffee can to the bottom of the pole, and buried it in the middle of the yard. All the neighbor kids came over to play tetherball, making a circular dirt patch in the yard. When another area of the lawn reached an undesirable length, up came the pole and over to the shaggy domain. Soon the entire lawn was a series of circular dirt patches. The aerial view of the lawn that year was impressive, and as we flew past, my dad never said "That'll teach 'em" out loud, but you got the feeling that's what he was thinking.

One evening, during dinner, Dad suddenly jumped up from the supper table. He was in the middle of his salad, "foliage" he called it, with vinegar and oil dressing. The perfect dressing for our family generally made your eyes water till you could knock back a glass of milk. Dad dropped his favorite fork, from the Navy, into his SpaghettiOs, made by the real Chef, "Boy-Ar-Dee," and ran outside cussing a blue streak. Our next-door neighbor, Ed Janish, was "accidentally" spreading fertilizer on our lawn.

"Your yard is nothing but dirt, Kling. It's a disgrace to the neighborhood."

"It's not what's on your lawn, it's what's in your heart, Ed."

"The lawn is the window to the heart."

My dad told Ed if he didn't stop fertilizing the yard, "Tomorrow, I'm going out and getting me a cottonwood."

The cottonwood tree. People in our area would rather have a convicted felon communist move in next door than a cottonwood. The Caughlin family, four blocks away, had a cottonwood, and once a year the prevailing winds filled the air with feathery parachutes, frosting the lawns with fertile little troopers. Ed Janish and the rest of the neighbors meticulously raked them up before they could breed, whispering a fate on Mr. Caughlin unparalleled since the Inquisition.

Ed says, "You are not."

Dad says, "I will, don't push me, Ed."

And the fertilizing stopped.

The next summer, Dad invested in another form of lawn maintenance. He pulled up the tether ball pole and came home with three guinea pigs.

"The only livestock this city will let a man have."

In two weeks' time, the three turned into six, then twenty, then fifty.

Dad appointed my brother and sister and me chief swineherds, and every day we would let the pigs out to graze. The lawn looked great that year, like a golf course.

In the winter months, the guinea pigs ran around in the basement in a huge wooden box. Every week or so we'd throw down some food pellets and a two-by-four board for them to gnaw on. It was an impressive sight to watch them whittle down a piece of lumber, and they loved the work. Every time they heard the basement door open their little voices would join in a squeaking chorus, "A board! Good God, a board is coming!"

That winter, the furnace went out. A service man came over to fix the boiler and when he opened the basement door, two hundred guinea pigs started screaming, thinking they were getting another two-by-four. A guinea pig does not make a fearful sound. It's like a little squeak. But in a pack, they can be daunting, and it's the closest living noise to the knife-wielding Norman screech from the movie *Psycho*.

The furnace man claimed, for religious reasons, he could not go into our basement. "With the Pope, maybe."

And we had to stay wrapped in blankets, freezing, until the furnace company sent a much more expensive atheist to fix our heat. Dad was upset at the inflated cost and made me stand guard to make sure the furnace man didn't take too many breaks. I helped speed up the process by holding the largest guinea pig, stroking him slowly, and whispering "Bad Kitty" the whole time.

The next summer we went back to the tetherball method of lawn care.

One day the phone rings.

"Kling, you really got to paint that house."

"Who is this?"

"A friend."

"Is that you, Janish?"

"No, it's not me. It's someone who cares about your standing in the neighborhood. For Heaven's sake, man, don't do it for yourself, do it for your children."

"Are these the same children you threatened to shoot with your twelve-gauge if they stepped foot on your lawn?"

"I wouldn't have to say that if they'd been trained to respect a man's property. And how are they going to learn to live in the world the way you keep your spread? It's a crying shame, Kling, and your children are going to be the ones to suffer for it."

"All right, Janish. Boys, we're going to paint the house."

"But Dad, it's a rental!"

"I know, boys, and it fries my ass to say this, but we live in a society where we have to learn to get along."

Mr. Janish is always frying my dad's ass. Other neighbors lightly sauté Dad's ass, but when it comes to a real frying, Ed Janish could really cook it up. "But Dad, we have to go play."

"Believe me, boys, I understand. Nobody likes to play more than I do, so we're gonna get that house painted in one day."

One day? That wasn't so bad.

"The whole house?"

My dad unveils his strategy.

He hands my brother a wire brush.

"Steven," he says, "take this and knock off all the loose dirt and paint around the house."

"Kevin, you take this newspaper and masking tape and cover all the windows."

Then my dad rents an air compressor and a spray nozzle attachment from a machine shop. Dad's plan is to clean up the house as best we can, and then "fire up" the compressor and spray paint all over the house in one giant sweep.

"I only got it for one day, boys." He shows us the invoice. "See there? Single day rental. That baby goes back tomorrow."

One day out of our lives doesn't seem so bad, and there's a built-in enthusiasm to see if Dad's plan can actually work.

"And," he continues, "if by some chance we finish by five o'clock, Teen Night!"

"Teen Night. Groovy."

Teen Night is a special treat. It's the night we pretend we're teens. It really means Mom doesn't want to be around during the aftermath of Dad's scheme, and his culinary skills end with hot dogs, canned baked beans, potato chips, and root beer, i.e., authentic teen food.

"Okay, Dad, we're in. What color we gonna paint it?"

"Well, boys," Dad says, "I don't know."

Dad is a manufacturer's representative for several industrial paint and pipe companies. His territory includes all of Minnesota and chunks of some neighboring states. A while back, Dad sold some paint for a water tower in northern Minnesota, and as was the custom, the contractor sent back the unused, unopened cans of paint. In this case, the job had been drastically over-bid, and hundreds of gallons of paint, all in five-gallon pails, now covered the garage from the oil spot to the back wall. Now, Dad couldn't remember what color that water tower had been painted, but that was the color our house was going to be. So he takes out a screwdriver and pops open a five-gallon pail and says,

"Well, boys, looks like we're painting her black."

Okay with us, it's still just one day.

My brother is off with the wire brush knocking off the loose dirt and paint. I come by hot on his heels with the newspaper and tape, and next my dad with the compressor, getting as much paint on the house as he can.

Midmorning, Grandpa and Grandma show up from Missouri. Whenever Dad launches into a major task it seems Grandpa comes running. Dad's plan is thoroughly approved by Grandpa, and now with an extra hand, we can go even faster. While Dad put Grandpa to work stirring paint, my brother and I sneak into the back yard to play. We start kicking a red inflatable rubber ball around in the back yard. Those balls that stay stinky no matter how old they get. As usual, a fight ensued, and my dad, hearing the commotion, comes running around the house, finds me crying in the back yard, and takes the ball away.

"I'll give you something to cry about."

And in one fantastic strike, he kicks the ball over the roof of the house. The three of us stand there for a moment in admiration. My brother and I know there will be no further punishment because of the distance of the kick. If Dad had shanked it or broken a window, then we would've been given more to "cry about," but clearing the house in one boot had taught us who we were dealing with, and that was good enough for now.

"Back to work."

When we get around to the front side of the house we find Grandpa covered in black paint, a bewildered look on his face, the rubber ball floating in the paint that remained in the five-gallon pail. Dad immediately looks straight up in the air, trying to spot the "SOB" who would do such a thing to Grandpa. My brother and I look at the earth. To meet Dad's or each other's eyes would mean uncontrolled laughter. We pick up the tools and without a word go back to work.

Dad proved true to his word, we finish the house in one day. In fact, we were finished by noon. We're ready to go play before "Teen Night." My dad says, "Wait a minute, boys, we still have that compressor another half day. Whaddaya say we do the trim?"

"Okay, Dad. What color is the trim?"

"Don't know."

We go into the garage and pop open another can.

"Well, boys, looks like it's going to be orange."

Before we are even finished with the trim, the neighbors are on the phone.

"It's primer, right? You're going to paint over it, right?"

Nope. That's the color we painted the house, and that's the color it will remain, because during Teen Night, Dad tells us, "That paint is the Cadillac of paint, boys. What we used today was a special graffiti-proof paint, made for when those junior high kids climb up the water towers to paint their names. Other forms of paint won't adhere to it. So as soon as it rains, their names will wash right off. So the next people to rent this house will paint it, which I know they will, and as soon as its rains"—his eyes get wide as he makes the sound of an approaching rainstorm then with his hands high over his head, fingers shimmering, he makes the sound of thunder and lightning, then in one downward sweeping motion his hands have becomes the new owner's paint job. "On the lawn," Dad says, and we all laugh, and I look over at Grandpa laughing with us on Teen Night, black "graffiti-proof" paint still dotting his bald head.

Kling with concertina, about 1990. (DAN CORRIGAN)

Kling and Mike Sommers in front of the Jungle
Theater, 1996, where "Waiting for Godot"
enjoyed a sold-out run. (MARY LUDINGTON)

A quiet moment, about 1995. (MARY LUDINGTON)

Acrobatics, about 1991.

From "Home and Away," which premiered at the Seattle Repertory Theater, 1991. (CHRIS BENNION)

FRANK THEATRE PRESENTS

Kevin Kling in

The EDUCATION of

WALTER KAUFMANN

Directed by Wendy Knox

The postcard for *The Education of Walter Kaufman*, produced in 1999 at the Frank Theatre, describes the play as "the sometimes charming, sometimes twisted story of a young man's education in the School of Life."

Guthrie Theater

Kevin Kling

TALES FROM THE CHARRED UNDERBELLY OF THE YULE LOG

Monday, December 15, 2003
at 7:30pm on the Thrust Stage

A postcard announced the annual holiday show at the Guthrie Theater in 2003.

I think the play was very funny. There
are only a few parts I did not understand.

I liked the part where he got struck
by lightning. It might be good for kids. Some
of the things I did not understand are the
parts about people.

A member of a school audience reacted to Kling's story about being
struck by lightning—like five other men in his family.

With Michael Sommers, director, on the Jungle Theater's set for
The Ice Fishing Play, 1994. (JOEY McLEISTER, STAR TRIBUNE)

THE ICE FISHING PLAY

Cast

Voiceovers or live
PAUL
TIM

Live
RON
IRENE
DUFF
BROTHER FRANCIS
BROTHER STEWART
JUNIOR

RON, DUFF and JUNIOR: men

IRENE: woman

BROTHER FRANCIS, BROTHER SHUMWAY, TIM, and PAUL can be a combination
of men and women

SCENE: The play takes place in an ice fishing house on a lake in northern Minnesota. The icehouse is about an eight-by-twelve-foot room. It has a stove, a
small table, and a cot that folds out of the wall; there are stuffed deer heads

and other animals and fish on the walls. There are also trap doors in the floor for fishing. When it's day, light comes from them. When it's night, they are dark. The house is not high tech, but it is very efficient, and comfortable. On the ceiling is a half-finished fresco, very good takeoff on the Sistine chapel, only God is reeling in a northern pike with cherubs cheering him on.

RON enters the icehouse. He is dressed for severe weather. As he opens the door, a storm is heard outside. His face is bright red; he has snow on his shoulders. In his hands are a bait bucket and a twelve pack of beer. He stomps his feet. *Sniffles stomp sniffle sniffle stomp sniffle sniffle stomp.* Takes the snow off his shoulders; wipes the red off his face. Walks to the stove, turns it on, takes off his snowmobile suit. Goes to the door marked Refrigerator, opens it. We see outside through the refrigerator door and hear the wind blow. RON throws the beer in. Then he turns on the radio. During TIM and PAUL's show, RON flips open one of the trap doors in the floor, takes out his ice auger, drills a hole, cleans the ice out, gets out a tip up—an ice fishing pole that shoots up a red flag when you have a bite—then he takes out a minnow, gives it a kiss, puts it on a hook, and drops it down the hole. Then he opens a beer, lights the stove, and sits down.

Part One

TIM: (*Lets out a blood-curdling SCREAM.*) AHHHH . . . turn it off, turn it off . . . OWWWW. Turn it off, Paul. Ow. Ow stop it . . . Jeez. Well, folks, all I can say is if it hurts like that on me, a human, just think what this baby will do to the fish. This is gonna revolutionize the sport, I tell you, Paul.

PAUL: Yeah, I'd say . . .

TIM: Whew. Well that little demonstration was courtesy of Junior Swansen's Fish Barn up there off Highway Ten and Lamont. You know, Paul, I was telling the wife last summer, I says, Passion, you've been working what, ten, twelve hours a day this whole week; what do you say we knock off and go fishing? SO naturally I take her down to Junior's for gear and bait. Old Junior is gone, you know, he traded in his Bassmaster and graphite rod for a harp three years back now, but his boy Junior the third, pound for pound probly the nicest guy you're ever gonna meet, has got that store decked out with all kinda these gadgets, and sonar, radar, bait—all your angling needs. Well, me and the wife, we set up by the shore in the shallows off this little weed bed till we seen some nice ones comin' in under the boat on the radar screen. An' before long, wham, bam, pow—they hit like tuna. Inside an hour we had our stringer crawlin' with a limit of three, four pounders. All keepers!

RON: Yeah, right.

TIM: Another true-life adventure brought to you by Junior Swansen's Fish Barn. You've tuned in to the Tim and Paul show, the eyes and ears of the North. I'm Tim, that's Paul, and together we're Tim and Paul.

PAUL: Yeah.

TIM: We're gonna have some fun today. No, not too much fun, Paul, just the right amount. SO let's see what we got for news. Oh jeez, you hate to see this. What's this world coming to, Paul?

PAUL: I don't know.

TIM: Topping our news coverage today: Police are out looking for the suspect in the failed robbery attempt at Jensen's Liquor Store. Nothing was reported missing in the incident, but the proprietor was shot three times in the chest. Police aren't releasing the name of the suspect, but he is reported in the area and is armed and dangerous. Jeez, what makes a guy do something like that? I don't get it, Paul, I just don't get it. Who would wanna shoot old Wiley Jensen three times in the chest, leaving his wife and two kids to run that liquor store by themselves, then not take anything, not even a bottle of something? You could understand it if the guy came up from the Cities, but from what I gather, he's a local boy for crying out loud—went to school with my own kid, was a track star, sung in the choir, for Pete's sake. Now he's out shooting up the town his father was the mayor of for twelve years . . . I don't know. The hackles on the neck are up, Paul. It's beyond me. *(RON kisses the minnow and puts it on the hook.)*

TIM: Seriously, folks, don't take any chances though, with this guy. He is a killer. He has killed. And he's around here somewhere . . . I tell you, these stories never get any easier.

(RON looks up at his gun rack.)

TIM: Let's move on to the weather, Paul?

PAUL: You bet.

TIM: Well, here we got some good news. There's an arctic express comin' in from Canada. It should hit any time today . . . Oh, jeez, look outside, Paul, it's already coming down like crazy. Wooow, look at that. It's been a while since I seen snow like this. Beautiful. Beautiful. Beautiful but deadly, folks. Look, we're in for a big one here—I mean, I can hardly keep from squealing like a child when I look at the weather report, but we gotta keep our heads. Stay inside. Lookee there at Paul. Paul's outta the studio now catchin' flakes on his tongue. Get in here, ya nut. I gotta admit, though, I never seen it snow like this since I was a kid. Now, if you're caught somewhere, stay put; if you have car trouble, wait by the vehicle till help arrives . . . Don't eat snow like Paul because, contrary to your thirst, it takes more energy than the liquid it provides. Pretend you're on the ocean and you can't drink the snow. Seriously, and be careful with alcohol—it'll thin your blood. I don't know about that really, but be careful because the dangers of hypothermia are real. Remember the rule, "If it hurts, you're doing fine, but if you start feeling good an' you're happy with yourself and your life seems nice and smooth, seek help immediately—that's hypothermia talking, something is wrong and you don't have much time."

Thanks, Paul. Paul, our mobile command weather unit, just handed me a bulletin. Wooow, heavens and earth, they're already saying this could be another Blizzard of the Century. That is as opposed to the Blizzard of the Century we had a couple years ago. And, oh boy, we've got some school closings coming up. Can you believe it? Paul, remember being a kid, all the family in the kitchen huddles around the radio for the school closings? An' now here we are, the bearer of glad tidings. While I read the list here, Paul, why don't you cue up that tape my son borrowed me and let her play, once again reflecting our effort to serve the needs of the entire community, as if to say, "Quit moving away you kids, there's a good life here."

Well here we go kids, listen up . . . Academy of the Holy Angel; Ada-Borup, private and parochial; Argyle, private and parochial; Astlby, private and parochial; Atwater Grove City, private and parochial; Austin, private and paro chial; Babbit, private and parochial; Badget, private and parochial; Barnsville, private and parochial; Barnum, private and parochial; Battle Lake, private and parochial; Beardsley-Valley, private and parochial; Becket, private and parochial; Belgrad-Brooten-Elrosa, private and parochial; Belle Plaine, private and parochial; Bemidji, private and parochial; Benson; private and parochial; Bertha-Hewitt, private and parochial; Bethlehem Academy, Bigfork, private and parochial; Big Lake, private and parochial; Blackduck, private and paro chial; Blaine, private and parochial; Blooming Prairie, private and parochial; Bloomington Jefferson, Bloomington Kennedy, Blue Earth, private and pa rochial; Bold, private and parochial.

(As TIM reads the list of schools, PAUL puts on music with a driving beat. RON's line goes under; the tip up jumps. RON sets the hook and starts to reel in.)

RON: Gotcha. I gotcha you bastard, haha . . . come on, baby, come on. Jeez, what a hog . . . come on . . . yeah, that's right. You're in the pan, you son of a bitch; you're on the wall of the rec room. I'm gonna fix it up just for you, you bastard, that's right—put up some nice paneling and a piece of shag carpeting over the oil spot on the concrete and a pool table and a bar and beer lights and a keg meister . . . (It's quite a fight.) NO. NO. No. No. No.

(All of a sudden the line is slack; RON pulls up a license plate. He looks at it. Throws it down. Stands and realizes something. Grabs the plate, looks at it again, and runs outside. He comes back in. His face is red and he has snow on him. He takes off the snow and wipes the red off his face. Takes his truck keys out of his pocket and drops them down the hole. RON turns off the radio. RON starts to bait another hook. LIGHTS up on IRENE.)

IRENE: I told you, Ron, din't I?

RON: Don't start on me now, Irene. I'm upset.

IRENE: I says, "Ronnie, you know that ice by the dam is too thin." And I told you I don't want to see you going out there.

RON: I know, Irene.

IRENE: Don't give me "I know." I know what "I know" means, and it doesn't mean, "I know"; it means shut up. Don't tell me to shut up Ronnie Huber—especially when you know I'm right. "I know." I want to see you get outta this one. You're dead this time, Ronnie. I swear. And I'll tell you another thing: if I find out you came out here, you can forget about coming home.

RON: Jeez, Irene. I come out here to be alone, so go on now. This is my place where I can go. I can have my peace of mind and listen to the radio, have a coupla beers if I want, and if something happens—say I sink my truck in the middle of a lake with maybe another Snowstorm of the Century movin' in—I can still look myself right in the eye and not feel like a dumb shit. That's why I got this place.

IRENE: All right. You want to be all alone, Ron?

RON: Yes.

IRENE: You want me to leave?

RON: Yes, I told you.

IRENE: All right, your wish is my command, Ronnie. Poof, you're all alone. (LIGHTS out on IRENE. RON sets another line, turns on the radio.)

RON: Good.

TIM: Braham, private and parochial; Brainerd, private and parochial; Brandon, private and parochial; Breckinridge, private and parochial; Brooklyn Center, private and parochial; Browerville, private and parochial; Brownton, private and parochial; Buffalo, private and parochial . . . *(There is a KNOCK-ING at the door.)*

VOICE OF FRANCIS: Hello, hello, is anyone home? Hello, I know you're in there, I can hear the radio. *(RON turns off the radio.)* I heard you turn it off. Hello.

RON: Burnsville, private and parochial; Butterfield-Odin, private and parochial; Byron, private and parochial; Caledonia, private and parochial; Cambridge, private and parochial; Campbell-Tinah, private and parochial; Canby, private and parochial; Cannon Falls, private and parochial; Carlton, private and parochial; Cass Lake–Bena, private and parochial; Cedar Mountain, private and parochial; Centennial, private and parochial; Chandler–Lake Wilson, private and parochial; Chaska, private and parochial; Chatfield, private and parochial; Chief Bug-O-Nay-Ge-Shig, private and parochial; Chisago Lakes, private and parochial; Chisholm, private and parochial; Chokio-Alberta, private and parochial; Clearbrook, private and parochial; Cleveland, private and parochial; Climax, private and parochial; Clinton-Graceville, private and parochial . . . *(More KNOCKING.)*

VOICE OF FRANCIS: Hello. *(RON answers the door. The wind is blowing.)* Good day, brother.

RON: Hey.

FRANCIS: My name is Brother Francis and this is Brother Shumway. *(There is a loud SNEEZE.)*

RON: Bless you.

SHUMWAY'S VOICE: Thank you.

FRANCIS: Could we trouble you for a minute of your time?

RON: Well . . .

FRANCIS: Please, brother. It's a matter of the utmost importance, Life and Death . . .

RON: Well, yeah, come on in. *(Brothers FRANCIS and SHUMWAY enter. They have red faces and cotton snow on their shoulders. During the next dialogue FRANCIS takes the towel, wipes off the red, and takes off the snow and puts it near RON's. SHUMWAY wipes his face, but the red won't come off; likewise the snow is sewn on his jacket and hat.)* You boys are out on a pretty raw night. Where are your coats? *(SHUMWAY SNEEZES.)*

RON: Bless you.

SHUMWAY: Thank you.

RON: Your buddy there seems to be in rough shape.

FRANCIS: Oh no, he's fine. He originally hails from a much more temperate climate, and your winters take a bit of getting used to.

RON: Well, you know we feel when you freeze paradise, it lasts a little longer.

FRANCIS: Yes.

RON: I'd offer you boys something, but all I got is beer.

FRANCIS: No, thank you, brother. *(Pause. SHUMWAY suppresses a sneeze.)*

RON: Well, whatya know for sure.

FRANCIS: The Grand Climax is at hand.

RON: Oh. You don't say. Now which Grand Climax is that?

FRANCIS: Brother, would you read this passage, please? *(FRANCIS shows RON a passage in a book.)*

RON: Happy is he who reads aloud and those who hear the words of prophecy, and who observe the things written in it; for the appointed time is near.

FRANCIS: Revelations 1:3. Can you tell me what that means?

RON: I gotta admit, I don't have a clue.

FRANCIS: Because your soul is not at rest, ready to comprehend the words of the Lord.

RON: No, I don't know because when I read aloud I gotta concentrate on the words, not their meaning, so I can't tell you what it means. Now if you were to let me read it to myself, I don't have to worry about all that. *(FRANCIS holds out the book. RON reads to himself.)* Well, apparently you're happy when it's time for your appointment?

FRANCIS: Good. Right. You're happy about an appointment. Now, brother, you do know who this is? *(Shows RON a photo in a book.)*

RON: Yeah . . . Oh, who is that? It's uh . . . it's, oh shit . . . it's right on the tip of my tongue . . . Godammit who is that . . . Christ, I outta know . . .

FRANCIS: It's Moses.

RON: No, that's not it. I know, it's Charlton Heston, that's who it is. Bird Man of Alcatraz.

FRANCIS: No.

SHUMWAY: That's Bert Lancaster.

FRANCIS: It's Moses.

SHUMWAY: I mean who played Bird Man of Alcatraz.

RON: No, Bert Lancaster, you're thinking of Barabbass.

SHUMWAY: That's Anthony Quinn.

RON: No, he's Spartacus.

SHUMWAY: Nope, Kirk Douglas.

RON: He's Sampson.

FRANCIS: It's Moses.

SHUMWAY: No, that's Victor Mature.

RON: No Victor Mature, that's Hercules.

SHUMWAY: Joe Bonamo was Hercules.

RON: I'll bet that was Joe Bonamo. Then the Bird Man of Alcatraz was Bert Lancaster. But this here, that's Charlton Hesston.

SHUMWAY: Right.

FRANCIS: IT'S MOSES! Moses, Moses. *(FRANCIS glares at SHUMWAY. SHUMWAY SNEEZES.)*

RON: Bless you.

SHUMWAY: Thank you.

FRANCIS: All right. Now brother, this time look carefully. Do you know who this is?

RON: Oh yeah, that's easy. That would be William Def . . .

FRANCIS: NO!

RON: All right, but I seen that one twice.

FRANCIS: Jesus. It's Jesus. Lord of Lords, King of Kings, Jesus. You've heard of Jesus?

RON: Of course I have, but you asked me who he was, not who he was playing.

FRANCIS: This is the real Jesus. Those are characters in movies. Not real. Movies. Particles of light. Written by people. Human interpretations and publications are fallible. Like Joseph of old would say . . .

SHUMWAY: Do not interpretations belong to God?

FRANCIS: Shumway, please.

SHUMWAY: Genesis 40:8.

FRANCIS: SHUMWAY. And please blow your nose. There are twenty-six letters in Our Lord's alphabet not twenty-four. (Back to RON.) Brother, I happened to notice you enjoying the fine art of fishing.

RON: Does the Pope . . . I mean is a nun's . . . Yeah.

FRANCIS: Did you know Jesus was also a fisherman?

RON: It only makes sense.

FRANCIS: And do you also recall the parable of the loaves and fishes, where Jesus fed five thousand people on two fish . . .

RON: *(To SHUMWAY.)* I'd give fifty bucks to see the game warden's face when he heard that one. *(RON and SHUMWAY crack up.)*

FRANCIS: Shumway, would you please wait for me outside?

SHUMWAY: Outside?

FRANCIS: Yes, until we're through here, please.

SHUMWAY: No.

FRANCIS: No?

SHUMWAY: No. I . . . I have a prayer.

FRANCIS: Very well, Brother Shumway, you may lead us in a closing prayer.

SHUMWAY: *(SHUMWAY loudly clears his throat.)* God, I don't understand. I know as God you cannot be understood except by yourself. So if we are to understand you we can only do so by being transformed into you, so that we know you as you know yourself. And since we will not know you as you know yourself until we are united into what you are. Faith seems to play a large role in this and . . . I . . . I don't know if . . . if I . . . *(SHUMWAY breaks down.)*

FRANCIS: It's all right, brother. In his name we pray.

SHUMWAY: Amen.

FRANCIS: Thank you, brother. Now wait for me outside. I'll only be a moment. *(SHUMWAY nods and exits.)* I don't think he's going to make it.

RON: Me neither.

FRANCIS: He doesn't have what it takes.

RON: Like a coat.

FRANCIS: Brother, am I not subjected to the same infirmities? Yet here I stand, strong and solid in my beliefs. Brother Shumway is weak because he doubts. Be that as it may . . . I will not quit his mission and soon he will be welcomed into the arms of Our Lord. I can guarantee Brother Shumway will have solace. Can you say the same? The apocalypse is near; there will be a judgment.

RON: It sounds more to me like the end of your Bible is near. Now go on and get out there, you nut, and bring your buddy back in here till the storm is passed. *(FRANCIS starts to exit. Stops.)*

FRANCIS: Brother Ron, I know why you are out here on this pristine lake void of life, this sanctuary.

RON: You do, huh?

FRANCIS: Yes. But you cannot escape, brother, for the devil you fear is not searching without; it lives within. The Lord sayeth, "The more we are alone the more we are together." Remember that, brother, one day death will knock upon that door . . . and on that day, Brother Ron, may your debts be paid in full and peace be yours. Good day. *(FRANCIS exits. The wind is blowing.)*

RON: WERE YOU BORN IN A BARN? *(RON closes the door.)* That kid's about fifty yards short of a full spool. *(He turns on the radio. It starts up—right where it left off.)*

TIM: Cloquet, private and parochial; Columbia Heights, private and parochial; Comfrey, private and parochial; Cook, private and parochial; Coon Rapids, private and parochial; Cosmos, private and parochial; Cretin–Derham Hall, Cromwell, private and parochial; Crookston, private and parochial; Dassel, Cokato, private and parochial; Dawson-Boyd, private and parochial; *(There is a KNOCK at the door. The radio stops on its own. RON looks at the door. TIM resumes.)* Deer River, private and parochial; Delano, private and parochial; De La Salle, Detroit Lakes, private and parochial; Denfield, private and parochial; Dover-Eyota, private and parochial; Duluth, private and parochial; Duluth East, *(There is another <u>KNOCK</u>. Silence. RON looks. TIM continues.)* Eagan, private and parochial; Eagle Valley, private and parochial; East Grand Forks, private and parochial . . . *(Another <u>KNOCK</u>. Radio is silent.)*

RON: Death?

VOICE OF DUFF: No, it's me, Duff. *(DUFF enters; the wind is blowing outside. He takes the towel and wipes the red off his face and puts his snow on top of RON's and FRANCIS's.)*

RON: Duffer, hey whatya know for sure?

DUFF: Takes a mighty big dog to weigh a ton.

RON: That's a fact. Cold enough for you?

DUFF: Yeah, I'd wear a coat. Any luck?

RON: Yeah, all bad. I lost my truck.

DUFF: I seen the hole. What did you lose?

RON: Chevy . . .

DUFF: You bought a Chevy truck? Ronnie! Slummin' it! How could you?

RON: What, I gotta good deal.

DUFF: I'd hope. *(DUFF sets up a line, kisses a minnow, hooks it, and drops it.)*

RON: Beer?

DUFF: What?

RON: You want a beer?

DUFF: No, thanks though. *(Long pause.)*

RON: It's been a while, Duffer.

DUFF: Twenty-seven years.

RON: Twenty-seven years. Jeez. *(Long pause.)*

DUFF: I ran into Irene. She says she's worried about you out here.

RON: She knows I am set up out here by the dam?

DUFF: Yeah, I guess. She told me right where to find you. *(LIGHTS up on IRENE reading a paper.)*

RON: Jeez, it's getting so I . . .

IRENE: Can't even finish a sentence without her knowing what I'm gonna say next.

RON: Seriously it . . .

It's like . . .

IRENE: I don't have a mind of my own sometimes.

RON: Heaven . . .

IRENE: And earth . . .

RON: I . . .

IRENE: Tell you.

RON: Why din't she come herself . . .

DUFF: She don't think you want her out here. *(They look at IRENE.)*

RON: Jeez.

DUFF: She's something, Ronnie.

RON: Sure is.

DUFF: Not from around here.

RON: No, south of here a ways, by the Cities.

DUFF: It's obvious. She's . . .

RON: Special.

DUFF: Yeah, I'm afraid so. Why don't you quit staring at her and go talk to her?

RON: I will.

DUFF: Well, go on then.

RON: I am. Irene?

IRENE: Yeah?

RON: Wanna go out with me?

IRENE: No.

RON: Goddamnit.

DUFF: Ahhh, shake it off, Ronnie.

RON: You din't see her up close, Duffer. If it gets any better I don't even wanna know about it. Jeez, she's a keeper, Duff.

DUFF: Then you gotta treat her like one. Present the bait, jog it a little. When you feel her tug, set the hook and get her in the boat. One two three. *(RON approaches IRENE.)*

DUFF: Be careful, though—she's special.

RON: Irene? Excuse me, Irene Hobbs.

IRENE: Cripes, it's cold.

RON: Well, you know how we feel when you freeze paradise, it . . .

IRENE: They're already calling it the Storm of the Century. What is that, the third Storm of the Century this year?

RON: You wanna go out with me?

IRENE: No, Huber.

RON: Hey, she knows my name.

IRENE: Storm of the Century, Man of the Year, Day of the Dolphin. If it ain't one thing it's another. Bears live here in the winter.

RON: Yeah.

IRENE: How do they do it?

RON: Well you see, they eat pine bark in the fall and the sap plugs 'em up, then in the spring they eat dogwood and whoosh . . . cleans 'em right out.

IRENE: No, how do they keep from going nuts up here?

RON: Oh, I don't know, maybe winter's the time they set aside to figure things out. So do you wanna . . .

IRENE: What is there to figure out?

RON: Well, like this conversation. However it turns out—which I already think I know how that'll be—I can go on the lake into my icehouse and sit and run through what you said and then what I said until it works out that I said the right things and you go out with me.

IRENE: Then what?

RON: Then I come back and try it again in person.

IRENE: What if I keep saying no?

RON: Then . . . well, then I guess sooner or later you gotta deal with my recessive gene.

IRENE: Your what?

DUFF: Not the recessive gene, Ronnie, you're gonna yank the hook right outta her mouth.

RON: Well, for some reason all of us Hubers—me, my ma, my dad, my brother Duffer—we'll be going along like anybody like nothing bothers us, when *Bam* . . . like a time bomb the recessive gene will kick in: we'll give in to an act of passion.

IRENE: I think you could stand to eat some dogwood, Huber.

RON: No. I'm serious. Ask anyone—it can be ugly. It's there from our past. It's something like Latin or Chippewa, just lurking in our weed bed.

IRENE: But I like you got it. You got a good heater in your truck?

RON: It's a Ford.

IRENE: Then come get me after school, Friday.

DUFF: Hey, Ronnie. Lookit this, Ronnie.

RON: What?

DUFF: They found two kids frozen to death already. Not ten feet from a house. I guess they were out doing missionary work and didn't see it coming. There's even a picture—look, the two of 'em frozen solid like a statue, one holding the other up like the Sands of Iwo Jima. Francis and Shumway. Poor guys—what were they thinkin'? Look, no coats or nothing.

RON: That's it—I knew I'd seen them before; they came up to the house on the last Storm of the Century. Francis and Shumway. Jeez. *(RON shudders.)*

DUFF: Schnapps?

RON: What? *(DUFF takes out a bottle.)*

DUFF: I got some schnapps. Takes the chill off. Here.

RON: Thanks. *(Takes a swig.)* Agh. Duffer.

DUFF: You like it? Plenty more where that come from.

RON: What is it?

DUFF: Sauerkraut. I made it myself. You can make schnapps out of anything, I found out. Just take your favorite flavor and add it in. *(Takes a swig.)* Ahhh. Perfect. I knew this guy once would put red pepper in his boots to keep his feet warm. Swore by it. Said if it worked in your mouth, it'll work on your feet.

Tried to get me to do it, but no way. I figure he tried it once, word got out, so in order not to look like a dumbshit he did it the rest of his life.

RON: No.

DUFF: Yeah, believe me, people go to great lengths to not look like a dumbshit when it's probly in their best interest to fess up and move on. *(Pause.)*

RON: All right! So I parked my truck by the dam! There, are you happy?

DUFF: I wasn't talking about you, Ronnie.

RON: No?

DUFF: No.

RON: I thought you were.

DUFF: I think you're a genius.

RON: Oh yeah, right. How do you figure that, Duff?

DUFF: Lookit, talent is something you're born with. God given. Can't do nothing about it. Smarts is something you gotta figure out on your own during life, but genius is something somebody else has to call you. You're a fishing genius.

RON: I have to break it to you, Duffer, but this lake we're sitting on ain't yielded so much as a crappie in five years now. I'm fishing on a dead lake, so don't make me out to be no genius.

DUFF: You know he's down there. That bastard's below us even as we speak, Ronnie boy, and you know it as well as I do. Why else would you sink your truck?

RON: That wasn't exactly on purpose.

DUFF: Sure, it's obvious, it's you or him and you're lettin' him know it the only way you can. I'm proud of you, lad . . .

RON: Duff, what if maybe I'm out here to relax, get away from it all? Did you ever think of that?

DUFF: Ronnie, people like you don't go fishing for no good reason. Do you think a man becomes a cop because he feels all is right with the world? Hell, no. Psychiatrists, you think they go into all that education because they wanna help other people? Hell, no—they got serious problems they need solving in their own heads . . . So, when you tell me you're out here just fishing, who the hell do you think you're talking to? I'll tell you, it's me, your brother Duffer, and there's a reason Dick Tracy is a cop, somebody is a psychiatrist, and you fish. Besides . . .

RON: What . . .

DUFF: You met the Old Man of the Lake.

RON: Yeah, I was a little kid, though.

DUFF: Don't matter. You were the only one to see him alive, right here on this spot. You hold his legacy.

RON: Naw.

DUFF: I was there when you came home. Boy, were you scared. An' when Dad got off work, we were waiting for him at the elevator. Remember? He came out of the mine with his hard hat and the light still on?

RON: He had to squint just to see who we were.

DUFF: But that squint—it wasn't just the sunlight he was getting used to, it was the world.

RON: And with me yelling "A monster, a monster . . . "

DUFF: You said there was a monster lived in the lake and that an old man told you. And Dad says, "Where'd you see that old man, son?"

RON: Out by the beaver dam.

DUFF: The beaver dam!

BOTH: I thought I told you . . .

DUFF: And then Dad beat you good from coming out here.

RON: Yeah, yeah he did.

DUFF: If you pull a fish up from the deep—and I'm talking about one of those ocean fish with a lantern on its head . . . if you pull one of those babies up too fast they explode, Ronnie, and you know why? It's because they're used to a different kind of pressure, see, a continuous amount. I always wondered what Dad was like in the mine, because the pressure of the outside world was not the one he was suited for . . .

RON: That's a fact. He went downhill fast when the mine closed up.

DUFF: Grampa got the trees. Dad got the iron ore. That left the fish.

RON: You should've stayed, Duffer. You could fish. Hell, you got the perfect build for it.

DUFF: You can teach a man how to bait a hook, but you can't teach him to fish. No. No, I had to get outta here. Face it, Ronnie, you're all we got left, Ronnie.

RON: We . . .

DUFF: And you gotta get that fish for me, you, Dad, Grampa, the Old Man of the Lake . . . All of 'em.

RON: All of who, Duff? *(Pause)* Duffer?

DUFF: We got on the ice at dawn. Cold. Cold to where your nostrils in your nose stuck shut if you breathed in through it. And quiet. Too quiet. We set up our portable canvas shacks, drilled our holes, and hunkered down. Nobody saying a word, nobody making eye contact for fear somebody will know what you're thinking, or, worse yet, you'll be thinking the same thing . . . "Did we bring enough bait? What if we're skunked? Don't say it or you'll jinx every-one." And we know the bastards are down there. But where is the question. How deep, what are they hitting on? I go with a leech on a jig; I'm a live bait man, you know, always was and I ain't ashamed of it. I hear the guy next to me, freckle-faced kid from the Cities, praying, I think it's to come through this with a nice keeper, but as I listen I hear him ask for the feeling of his toes back . . . Poor kid, but did he ever mention it, or wanna go back and warm up in the truck? Hell, no, that's the caliber of the men I was with, Ronnie.

Then at oh-three-hundred they hit. Oh God, did they hit. For most of us, it was the first tournament we'd ever seen. And here they come, school after school. Hitting one wave after another. All keepers . . . I think, no, no. What am I say-ing? There were perch mixed in there, rough fish, little ones we shoulda been throwing back, but it came so fast—bam pow—there was no time to think, no time to identify . . . throw 'em on the ice and rebait the hook. We'll sort 'em out later . . . No time to get the gloves back on; I couldn't feel my fingers, Ronnie. I know it sounds like utter chaos, but in the midst of it all there we were, a bunch of guys who a week ago didn't know each other from Adam, working together like a well-oiled machine . . .

And then I hear it like a hole in the confusion, a lone voice, "The bait's not gonna last . . . we're low on leeches and minnows both." Well, there's no time to go to the gas station and get more bait—the school will be long gone by then. Raymond Welsh looks up from the minnow bucket. "That's it," he says. "This is the last one." We draw straws and they give the last minnow to me . . . "You know he's down there, Duff, we need the big one or it's no trophy. Come on, Duffer," I baited up and lowered him down . . .

RON: What happened, Duffer?

DUFF: Let's just say we forgot the number-one rule. Never enter a tournament you know you can't win. But I guarandamntee there's never been another one like it, and I guess there never will be. *(DUFF takes a swig of schnapps.)*

RON: God. I wish I woulda been there.

DUFF: No you don't, Ronnie.

RON: That wasn't really a fishing story.

DUFF: No, but I thought I'd put it in a way you could grasp.

RON: I miss you, Duff.

DUFF: Don't say that.

RON: I do, though.

DUFF: Yeah, but you don't say it, jeez, Ronnie. Besides, I'll be back.

RON: You said that the last time.

DUFF: And here I am. *(DUFF heads for the door.)* I'll tell Irene you're fine.

RON: Thanks.

DUFF: Later.

RON: Later. *(DUFF exits. LIGHTS up on IRENE reading the paper. RON doesn't notice her. IRENE looks at RON. He still doesn't notice. The radio starts.)*

TIM: Irene Hobbs, private and parochial; Irene Hobbs, private and parochial; Irene Hobbs, private and parochial; Irene Hobbs, private and parochial; Irene Hobbs, private and parochial . . . *(RON notices IRENE.)*

RON: Irene? Irene?

IRENE: Hmmmm.

RON: What ya reading?

IRENE: *(Straight faced.)* The funnies.

RON: The funnies?

IRENE: Well, first I got in the habit of it because they sit there just above the horoscopes. And with you out fishing on the lake all the time, I'd get out the paper and read the horoscopes to see how your day is out there. What you're thinking and what you're doing, who you're having an affair with . . .

RON: I'm fishing . . .

IRENE: And then one day I seen an ad for this art colony that says I might already have talent. And they have this test where I can draw the famous head of Tippy the Turtle, Pete the Pirate, Carl the Carp, or a split-level condominium. So I go with the carp for luck and two weeks later I get back a letter and, lo and behold, Ronnie, I've got talent.

RON: I know that. You coulda saved yourself a stamp.

IRENE: Yeah, but when it comes to art you like to hear it from a professional.

RON: I spose.

IRENE: Anyhow, since I have proven talent it turns out I am privy to a list of courses to take, like Secret Expert Tips of the Masters; Exploring New Art Methods; From Doodles to Dollars. And this whole other world opened up to me, Ronnie. I gotta tell you this excitement started welling up that I haven't had since I was in high school and did something on my own. You know, completely on my own. And look, here they give a list of graduates from the program . . . some of these people are really famous . . . like this guy here. He's a graduate of the art colony. That mountain looks real enough to climb, huh?

RON: I wonder where that mountain is.

IRENE: By the colony, I guess. And that's not all. Look, here's a guy who does internal organs for medical journals, and here's somebody who draws fashion illustrations, and another one who drew Mickey Mouse for forty-five years, and this guy here is in the funnies every day. See, here he is in today's. So, anyhow, I was just lookin' at the funnies to see if maybe that's my particular area of expertise.

RON: I don't wanna pop your bubble, Irene, but those things are scams. They just want your twenty bucks.

IRENE: Fifty.

RON: Fifty—that can't be right. Fifty bucks for art school?

IRENE: Ronnie, it's got a reputation, and besides, I figure if I even sell three or four paintings I'll make that back easy.

RON: Well, alls I got to say is if you want to take up art, take up a real art.

IRENE: Like what?

RON: Christ, Irene, like taxidermy.

IRENE: Taxidermy!

RON: Don't laugh; it's an ancient art that honors the hunt.

IRENE: I don't want to kill for my art, Ron.

RON: I'll kill 'em. I'd be happy to if that will give you something to do. Look, we'll set you up in the basement, I'll put up some nice paneling, put a piece of shag carpet over the oil stain . . . besides, if you get good we can set it up as a bonus for people who hunt and fish out of the resort. Bring in some extra cash.

IRENE: I'm not sure about this one.

RON: Don't call it short, Irene. Vanity is a powerful thing. There was a guy come up here from the Cities. Boat, motor, all brand-new equipment. Says he sold makeup during the war, made a fortune. Told me that during good times or bad, people want to look good. In fact, oftentimes they'll go without food before makeup.

IRENE: I can see that.

RON: Well, a nice walleye over the mantel is to a guy what lipstick and eyeshade is to a woman, you know, in that it revolves around the vainness of a man's masculinity.

IRENE: All right, so?

RON: So alls I'm saying is why mess around with the funny papers when you can have the real Carl the Carp?

IRENE: You'd have my ass if I put a carp on the wall.

RON: All right, then, Nathan the Northern, William the Walleye, Mark the Muskie. Huh? I'll even sweeten the pot and throw you a big party for your first deer head.

IRENE: I don't want a deer head party. Lookit, Ronnie. I sit around here day after day while you're outside fishing.

RON: I don't know what to tell you, Irene. You should get out more if you want, or visit with Cookie Crumbfelter.

IRENE: Ron, I gotta tell you, I ain't all that fond of Cookie. We got different interests. All's she cares about is . . . she says, "Isn't this dress fun?" Fun? I was brought up thinking fun revolved around an activity, but I go along with her and says, "That's a nice one, Cookie. It looks really fun, a blast." "Oh," she lets out a big sigh, "I don't know." Like it's gonna be a problem somewhere down the line. I swear, Ronnie, I don't think that woman is happy unless she's depressed. Or she says, "I seen a movie." All right, Cookie, what movie? . . . Well, she don't remember, but it was about a man who was . . . oh, what's that actor's name, oh you know who I mean, he has a father, who had a friend, that lived in . . . oh, what's that town's name . . . oh, who was he, he had the hair . . .

RON: That would be Joe Banamo in Hercules.

IRENE: How did you know that?

RON: It's obvious.

IRENE: Well, then, you should talk to Cookie. Don't make me.

RON: All right, Irene, jeez. Join the damn art colony. I just think it's a rip-off, and that's my honest opinion.

IRENE: BUT THAT DON'T MATTER. *(Pause.)* When I was in high school I had this feeling. It was this sensation where I could step outside myself and look at how I fit in the world. And it didn't revolve around another human. It was pure, like a primary color, like yellow. It was just I in the world. And then I met you and you sort of set up house in that feeling, but I didn't mind—that's right were I wanted you. Then we had Darlene and naturally it fell to me to do most of the raising, but I didn't mind that either because, believe me, I love her with all my heart.

RON: God, she was a pretty baby.

IRENE: She looked like a boy, Ron. I had to scotch-tape bows to her head so people din't call her "little fella." Anyhow, over time I forgot I was getting older, and now in the winter Darlene's in school, the resort's all closed up, and you're out on the lake, and what do I do, Ron? I got so many colors mixed in there I don't know how to get yellow back.

RON: I don't know what to tell you, Irene.

IRENE: Well, what about you?

RON: What?

IRENE: Don't you want something, Ron?

RON: Like what?

IRENE: Don't you have dreams?

RON: Sure I do . . . like what, though?

IRENE: Well, what would you wish different for your life?

RON: Let's see. I got this place, the resort keeps us above water, I gotta nuff to help to where I can fish, especially in the winter. The bar keeps us eating, and I've only had two fights in there; I been in both of 'em. I gotta beautiful wife and a daughter who sort of looks like me, but not enough to make me worry about her future.

IRENE: But that's what you already got.

RON: Yeah? I'm happy, Irene.

IRENE: Isn't there something you want to do or be or go?

RON: Yeah, I guess I'd like to go somewhere, but where? I'm not missing anything by living out here, and even if I am, I don't know what it would be. I'm sorry, but I'm happy, Irene.

IRENE: What do you want? Then what is it that bothers you, huh? What, Ronnie. There must be something I do. What is it?

RON: Nothing. Now don't try to get me upset just because you know how.

IRENE: Ronnie, what is it?

RON: There's nothing.

IRENE: What? Then what scares you?

RON: Irene, I'd just be making something up.

IRENE: What scares you then? What Ronnie?

RON: Nothing.

IRENE: What, Ronnie, what what?

RON: One thing?

IRENE: Yeah, what?

RON: I'm afraid . . . let's see . . . I'm afraid to be alone.

IRENE: That's not it.

RON: It is.

IRENE: That can't be it. You're alone all winter. I hardly ever see you.

RON: That's not the same "alone." I always know where you are. I always know I can find you if I need to. So I'm not alone. Look, in the winter, how long am I on the ice in one stretch?

IRENE: You come in every four days. I could set a clock by it.

RON: That's how long I can last, four days, and then I gotta get in and see you and make sure you're here.

IRENE: Jeez, Ronnie, of course I'm here, where else would I be?

RON: I'm not saying it's realistic; I'm just saying it's a fear I got. When Duffer was serving overseas he wrote me this one time. He said when he'd go on leave, for R and R, they'd get to go into Hong Kong sometimes, in China. He said there's a custom there that if a woman dies before she's married, her folks would take some of her things, her most prized possessions, and put 'em in a box, then leave the box by the side of the road. If you were a gentleman and unattached and you came upon one of these boxes, you had the option of picking it up and going to a church and marry the young woman. Your souls are then joined in heaven, and from then on you are never alone. He said sometimes he felt like taking one of those boxes and getting married just in case something happened to him, but he never did. He was killed shortly after I got that letter, and with the funeral and grieving and all it slipped my mind what he'd written. I found that letter a couple of years ago, and I took Duffer's chainsaw, his lucky hat . . . put 'em in a box, left 'em off Highway 7. A week later I drove by and, lo and behold, it was gone.

IRENE: That was a nice thing you did for your brother.

RON: Sometimes I wonder, though, if some old guy came by and seen it—"free chainsaw"—and little does he know now he's married off to Duffer.

IRENE: It don't matter.

RON: That's what I thought. Without sounding too liberal minded, I figured a soul was a soul, and if Duff is pissed off he'll let me know soon enough. And on the flip side, it'd serve the old geezer right for taking a chainsaw that doesn't belong to him.

IRENE: Did you ever get the feeling Duff didn't like me?

RON: Why do you say that?

IRENE: Well, when we got married, what was his gift? A year's supply of bait at Junior's Fish Barn. And then he goes and writes "Just Married" on the car with bumper stickers that say, "I'd rather be fishing."

RON: Oh, he was just joking, Irene. That was his way.

IRENE: Maybe to the naked eye, but there was always something with us.

RON: I wouldn't lose any sleep over it. *(IRENE comes into RON's icehouse.)*

IRENE: Well, don't you worry, Ronnie Huber, you will never be alone. Ever. That I can promise with all my heart.

RON: I think you should take that art colony.

IRENE: I didn't mean to go off on Cookie like that.

RON: I know. I thought you were going to make a comment on her lips, though.

IRENE: Why no, Ron, I wasn't gonna say anything about her lips.

RON: Oh.

IRENE: What about 'em?

RON: They always amaze me they're so . . . thin. Looked like rubber bands to me. In fact, when we were little I used to pretend me and her were married and I would take a rubber band and practice making out.

IRENE: Did you like it?

RON: No.

IRENE: Good. I'll tell you what, Mr. Huber, if you foot the bill for one week at the art colony . . . I'll give a whirl at stuffing the next Nathan or William or Mark you pull out of the lake. Deal?

RON: Deal. On one condition. No more talk of art tonight, all right Irene?

IRENE: All right, Ronnie, no more art.

TIM: Ellsworth, private and parochial; Elko, private and parochial; Ely, private and parochial; Eveleth, private and parochial; Fairmont, private and parochial; Faribault, private and parochial; Farmington, private and parochial; Fergus Falls, private and parochial; Fertile-Beltrami, private and parochial; Fisher, private and parochial; Floodwood, private and parochial; Foley, private and parochial; Fond du Lac Ojibway, Forest Lake, private and parochial; Fosston, private and parochial . . .

(_BLACKOUT._ *End of Part One.*)

Part Two

SCENE: *Back in the icehouse, RON is asleep on the cot. The deer head has a party hat on and a cigarette in its mouth. The radio is playing a polka. RON is sleeping with a smile on his face, but as the commercial progresses into tropical themes his dream turns into a nightmare.*

TIM: *(There is the _SOUND_ of a severe winter storm.)* Sound familiar? *(The _SOUND_ of a car that won't start.)* Winter got you down? *(Tropical Hawaiian _MUSIC_ plays.)* Hey, then give a call over to Backwoods Excursions for all your traveling needs . . . Hawaii, the Bahamas, Puerto Vallarta; beautiful beaches; tropical foods, shopping, exotic floorshows; palm trees; the sun; friendly natives; fruit; swimming; scuba diving; snorkeling; sightseeing; volleyball, horseback riding; surfing; hiking; dune buggies; coconut sculpture. *(DUFF enters quickly so as not to make too much noise with the wind outside. He turns off the radio; RON is in the throes of a nightmare, saying "No, no" and repeating themes like "volleyball," and "snorkeling." DUFF takes a fish—a large mounted northern pike—off the wall, pulls up RON's line, puts the fish on the hook, and lowers it down. Then he flips the tip up so the red flag is up.)*

DUFF: Ronnie, hey, wake up in there, wake up . . . Your bobber's under . . . You gotta fish . . . *(RON gets up; he is drowsy. He goes to the line as if on automatic pilot.)*

RON: What?

DUFF: You got a fish, Ronnie. Set the hook. *(RON sets the hook.)*

DUFF: You got him.

RON: I got him. Come on, you bastard, you're on the wall now. In the room with the paneling and carpet. Woooo, he's a heavy one.

DUFF: Play him, Ronnie.

RON: Like a log; not much of a fighter.

DUFF: Don't give him slack.

RON: I know.

DUFF: You got him, that's for sure. They'll get sluggish in the winter.

RON: Yeah, that they will. Come on baby, come on, come on . . . *(RON pulls up the mounted fish.)*

DUFF: Not a lot of meat on him, but he'll look nice on the wall. Here's a spot.

RON: Real funny, Duff.

DUFF: You shouldn't have been sleeping, anyhow. If that was the real hog, you woulda lost him.

RON: God, I had a nightmare. Volleyball.

DUFF: Hey, I got a surprise for you. *(DUFF goes to the window and peeks out.)* Shhhhhh. Look.

RON: Hey, it's Junior! What the hell is he doing?

DUFF: Standing on his head.

RON: Why? He looks stupid.

DUFF: I convinced him it would be funny if you opened the door and there he was standing on his head in the middle of the Storm of the Century.

RON: It does look pretty funny! *(RON goes to open the door.)*

DUFF: Wait; let's see how long he can hold it.

RON: I never figured Junior to be so nimble. *(They observe JUNIOR out the window. Long pause.)* Whoops.

DUFF: There he goes. Quick. He's gonna be madder than a bear with a sore ass. *(They go to the door; DUFF swings it open.)* SURPRISE, JUNIOR. What you laying there for? Get in here, you doof. *(JUNIOR enters. He is covered with snow and has a red face. He takes off the snow and wipes the red off his face. RON and DUFF hide behind the fridge.)*

DUFF AND RON: Surprise!

DUFF: Junior, is that a tube of Chapstick in your pocket, or are you just happy to see me? Junior, I thought you were gonna be standing on your head?

JUNIOR: Thanks for holding out so long, Duff. While I'm out there freezing my ass off. You aren't as smart as you think, either. I seen your little eye peeking out the window behind the curtain. Hey, Ronnie, news flash: your brother's an asshole.

RON: Tell me about it. *(He reaches out his hand.)* Put-er in the vice, Junior. *(JUNIOR shakes it.)*

JUNIOR: Here's the five I owe ya. Got a beer for me?

RON: There's a square in the fridge.

DUFF: It's nine in the morning, Junior.

JUNIOR: So? Run with the dogs or piss with the pups, Duffer.

RON: Grab two.

DUFF: Three. *(JUNIOR goes to the fridge.)*

RON: How's the wife, Junior?

JUNIOR: Cookie? Fine. Irene?

RON: Fine.

JUNIOR: Think fast. *(JUNIOR throws the can to DUFF.)*

She still doing taxidermy?

RON: Not much call for it, anymore. So she's been painting. Always liked painting better, anyhow. She's good too, boy, real good, like a photograph.

JUNIOR: Let me know if she tackles another deer head. I swear that deer head party was the best party of the year. *(JUNIOR and DUFF and RON open up their beers and hold them high.)*

RON: Cheers.

DUFF: To your health.

JUNIOR: Pork chop in every can. *(They all take a swig.)*

JUNIOR: Jeez, Pabst. Ronnie, give a skunk a job.

RON: You're welcome, Junior. *(JUNIOR starts doing a strange dance.)*

DUFF: What are you doing, Junior?

JUNIOR: I got red pepper down my leg from standing on my head. So whatya know for sure?

RON: What's it look like, I'm sitting around practicing for when I get old?

JUNIOR: No luck, huh?

RON: Nope.

JUNIOR: What ya using?

RON: Jig and shinner minnow.

JUNIOR: You guys and your live bait. I'm telling you, the fish are way ahead of you. They don't fall for live bait anymore.

DUFF: Junior, tell me, what do fish eat when we're not fishing?

JUNIOR: That's not my point. Fish are wiser now. They actually know when you're fishing, so live bait is basically ineffective. You gotta give 'em something they can't resist, that goes beyond their common sense. Something with a battery in it.

DUFF: Let me guess. Something that goes for fifteen dollars at Junior's Ripoff Barn.

JUNIOR: Have your fun, but you can't argue with genetics.

DUFF: You're so educated, you're stupid.

JUNIOR: Look, it's simple evolution. All the fish that are moronic enough to get caught are nailed at two or three pounds . . . but the smart ones, the ones that live to spawn, create the future generations . . . Hey, they don't even know they're smart; it just gets passed on because they lived.

DUFF: You make me thankful I'm not a reader.

JUNIOR: Look. Here's an extreme case scenario. Let's say there's a fish that, totally by accident, when it is subjected to oxygen, makes a noise that sounds like, "Release me and I'll grant you three wishes." I'll bet my beer can collection that over an amount of time there's gonna be a lot of those fish, let me tell you. And they can't even give the three wishes. Hell, they don't even know what they said, but the fact they said it ensures the survival of their race. Here's a real example. Where are all the muskies? I'll tell you where. Gone. Why? Stupid.

DUFF: Junior, you're like Lake Mille Lacs—you're not very deep and you go on forever.

RON: What about pollution?

JUNIOR: There are fish they could introduce . . . they eat pollution; they love it like candy, can't get enough of it. Science has known this for years, but some bleeding-heart purist somewhere got to 'em first. I'll tell you, though, any year now these lakes could be teeming again.

DUFF: You've been running a bait store too long.

JUNIOR: And I'm gonna keep running it. It's the same with humans, you have to evolve or die out, but I'm not talking physically now; I'm talking fiscally.

RON: Which holds by your same law of the jungle theory.

JUNIOR: Is a pig's butt pork? I was over at Wiley Jensen's liquor store the other day, and he's got a screen door leaning up against a stack of twelve packs. Next day a pile of screen doors. I ask, "What's going on, Wiley? Where'd you get all the screen doors?" He says they're from the people livin' in government housing. He's giving a twelve pack for every screen door and word got out. Hell, he's gonna make a bundle sellin' 'em off come summer.

RON: I don't like that.

JUNIOR: Why? It's government housing; they got all the doors for free.

DUFF: He shouldn't be making deals like that. He's gonna get his one day, that guy, somebody's gonna finally snap and take him out, mark my words.

JUNIOR: He's just making a living. Times are hard.

RON: Not that hard. Besides, the last time times were hard Wiley put an addition on the store.

JUNIOR: Whereas you buy a resort and the fish stop biting, what got? You're screwed, Ronnie. No offense, but I think you're just jealous.

DUFF: What about the Fish Barn?

JUNIOR: The Fish Barn will always be there because we diversify. We keep ahead of the times, give people what they want before they know they want it, and that's why my kid Junior the third is gonna be fine too. Genetics. He's like the son of that fish that survived even though it didn't know what it said. And while you Huber boys are mulling over that one, I'll be right back. (JUNIOR heads for the door marked with the sticker for unisex restroom.)

DUFF: Wait up.

DUFF: I gotta go, too. Sword fight.

JUNIOR: Then you go on. I'll be next. I was down in the Cities one time with my old man. He was down there on some union business for the mine, so he took me along, and when he was done we went to a ballgame down at Miller's field. I'm in the men's room standing at the trough and I'm just starting to go when I look up and this old guy is staring at me. And he's smiling—just his lips, no teeth—and for some reason I couldn't go, and ever since I can't go in front of another human. It's a fact, and sometimes if I think somebody can hear me I have to make up mental games to get going.

RON: Like what?

JUNIOR: I have to pretend I enjoy it. Like I'll say over and over, "I like to go in front of men. I like to go in front of men." Like a chant.

RON: And that works?

JUNIOR: Most of the time.

DUFF: I don't believe it.

JUNIOR: It's true.

DUFF: I believe it's true. I don't believe you told us.

JUNIOR: Hey, I got nothing to hide. *(He exits.)*

RON: I think sometimes it's best to have a few things to hide.

DUFF: Yeah, me too. *(Pause.)*

JUNIOR'S VOICE: Hey, cut it out.

DUFF: What?

JUNIOR'S VOICE: I know you're listenin' in there.

DUFF: Don't forget to dot the "i," Junior.

JUNIOR'S VOICE: Talk about something.

RON: Like what?

JUNIOR'S VOICE: I don't know; pretend I'm not out here. Hurry up, I gotta go.

DUFF: That Junior, what a dumbshit.

RON: I tell you, if stupid had weight he'd have been through the ice a long time ago.

JUNIOR'S VOICE: No, something else.

DUFF: I like to go in front of Duff and Ron.

RON AND DUFF: I like to go in front of Duff and Ron.

JUNIOR'S VOICE: Come on.

DUFF: All right Junior. *(Quieter.)*

DUFF: What is it with Junior?

RON: What?

DUFF: He seems his old abrasive self, but then he goes and admits something like this and I get worried.

RON: Lost his dog.

DUFF: Ran off?

RON: Died.

DUFF: That big black lab? Happy, stupid old lab?

RON: It made the mistake of saving Junior's life . . . starting barking the night the original Fish Barn burnt down. Junior got up to yell at it like he did every night and then saw the flames. He swore the dog warned him, and then Junior was so grateful he set the thing up in the lap of luxury. I mean that dog had its own place setting at the dinner table, had its own bunk beds, a beanbag chair in front of the TV. The poor thing started getting fat. I swear the only exercise it got was when it was dreaming. He stopped barking; started getting tumors like a human. I tell you the thing forgot it was a dog . . . and I told him, I says, "Junior, you gotta let Tuffy be a dog. Get him outside." So he took it fishing; bought it gear and a sweater and even drilled it a hole. In under ten minutes Tuffy's bobber went under and the dog went in the hole right after it. Junior grabbed for him but just got the sweater.

DUFF: Tragic.

RON: Junior swears he heard the dog come up in another icehouse and the people could tell quality and stole it. But I personally think Tuffy committed suicide. Anyhow, it's still a sore spot between me and Junior because I talked him into taking Tuffy fishing. *(JUNIOR enters.)*

DUFF: All finished?

JUNIOR: Yep. *(Pause. They stare at JUNIOR.)*

JUNIOR: What? Who needs a cold one?

RON: I do.

DUFF: I do.

JUNIOR: What are you two dumbshits fishing in a dead lake for, anyhow? *(JUNIOR goes to the refrigerator and gets three beers.)*

DUFF: It ain't a dead lake, Junior. There's still one left down there, a monster.

JUNIOR: Yeah, right.

DUFF: The one that got the Old Man.

JUNIOR: The Old Man, that's just a legend.

DUFF: Ronnie seen the Old Man on his last night alive right here on this spot.

JUNIOR: That so, Ronnie?

RON: Yeah, I was little, though; I don't remember so good.

DUFF: Listen up, Junior; this lake was formed by the glaciers and is by far the deepest in these parts, and combined with the beaver dam there are depths to this pool that can't even be hit with your sonar. There's an Indian legend that a creature lives in the center of this pit. A ravenous beast, eyes bulging with grief, a serpent's body, and a luminous beacon suspended from its forehead. Now, some demons can be bought off with prayers and gifts, but this one requires blood.

JUNIOR: Jeez.

DUFF: It's said the Old Man was half Indian, half French, big of bone, his face innocent in feature and expression. Poison Roy the Fisher King. Raised by the mild of wild beasts yet refusing to build with poplar wood because that was the tree they used to crucify Jesus. He was pure in all ways; in fact, he had no scent, couldn't be tracked. Poison Roy, the last one to fish here by the dam, swore he would land this fish, and this is what Ronnie walked into that night.

JUNIOR: You don't have a choice, Ron. You hold his legacy.

RON: Yeah.

JUNIOR: Don't matter, Ronnie, you inherited the hog.

DUFF: He knows it. Ronnie?

RON: Why do you think I sunk my truck?

JUNIOR: Brilliant.

DUFF: All right.

JUNIOR: Hey, if anybody can bring that fish in, it's the combination of these three great minds.

DUFF: I swear, Junior, you're an embarrassment to the man you think you are.

JUNIOR: Don't think you're so high and mighty, Huber. You get in your bass boat one leg at a time, just like the rest of us. I got smarts. I know every plug that's been invented. Now, I'll admit you got a talent to get people, fish, I don't care what, to do things they'd never dream of doing, and Ronnie . . .

DUFF: Is the fishing genius.

JUNIOR: If that bastard's down there, we'll get him.

DUFF: He's down there all right, and Ronnie's gonna haul him in.

JUNIOR: Well, if he hasn't bit a minnow and jig all these years, he's not gonna start now.

RON: Junior's right. *(JUNIOR opens RON's tackle box.)*

JUNIOR: Now for the perfect bait. Lemme see. What all you got here? Got a White Lighting Swedish Pimple Mud Puppy Lady Luck Go for the Gold Touchdown Medusa's Head Kiss Me I'm Irish Win Place or Show Chug-A-Lug Hula Princess Afterlife in the Weed Bed.

DUFF: What's this one, Junior?

JUNIOR: I'll be, that's an old Enticer. Jeez, I haven't seen one of those in a while. A classic.

RON: Oh, that was a gift from Irene when we first started going out. I'll never forget. I laughed at it and hurt her feelings, so I hung on to it so she could see it in my tackle box. I never used it. *(JUNIOR and DUFF look.)*

DUFF: That's the ticket.

RON: Naw, you guys.

JUNIOR: Look, over the years that fish has had a shot at everything in this box ten times over, but I guarandamntee one thing, it's never met up with an Enticer.

DUFF: Put a minnow on it.

JUNIOR: That's sacrilege. Live bait on the Enticer? Look, you already got yer battery-powered wiggle action. We'll spray on a little "Scent Away" human smell repellent. *(JUNIOR sprays some on.)* Don't get this stuff near your beer or you'll taste fish till you can get your teeth brushed. There, we're all set.

DUFF: Put a minnow on it.

JUNIOR: A minnow, what the hell for?

DUFF: Look, I say we don't take any chances. *(Kisses the minnow.)*

JUNIOR: You kissed the minnow. Are you superstitious or what?

DUFF: No, but I don't wanna jinx it this late in the game. It's common sense.

JUNIOR: But you put the human smell on it. *(JUNIOR sprays the minnow with "Scent Away" human smell repellent.)*

JUNIOR: There, all set.

RON: Looks good, Junior.

DUFF: No, wait. We gotta face facts. There's a chance the lad is already freezing to death.

RON: I never felt better.

DUFF: Now you do, but we need to give you an edge in case you get woozy . . . I got it. We'll make an addition on this tip up. *(DUFF gets down the shotgun and cocks the gun.)* We jerry-rig it so when the hog bites, it pulls the trigger. Bam, the gun goes off and wakes you from your slumber . . . You might miss a tip up flag, but if you got any consciousness, you won't miss a gun going off. All right, Ronnie, I loaded in two shells so if the first one don't wake you up you got one more. Then muster whatever strength you got left and haul him in. *(In the meantime JUNIOR has added more hooks to the Enticer.)*

RON: What're you putting on there, Junior?

JUNIOR: We're gonna nail this bastard. I got everything on here but the kitchen sink.

RON: Isn't that gonna tear him up?

DUFF: Nope, he won't feel a thing.

JUNIOR: He's right—fish don't feel like people. Most animals don't. *(DUFF is rigging the shotgun to the tip up.)* Fish don't feel like we do. Cut a fish in two, it'll just swim along no pain on its face. They're not like . . . a monkey . . . they're smart. I seen this one show where the scientist taught a monkey how to smoke. Some of the apes are almost as smart as humans, and there was this dolphin.

RON: Taught him how to smoke?

JUNIOR: No. What good is smoking gonna do a dolphin? No, they taught them a language, like radar, but a dolphin is not a fish, mind you. A mammal. A fish don't feel like us. Only monkeys and dolphins and some strains of dogs. A good dog; not yappy ones.

RON: Chickens?

JUNIOR: No. We eat chickens. Chickens.

DUFF: Now, all right, we're all set. When he takes it you're gonna know it . . . Be sure to keep your head clear of the barrel. Keep an eye peeled. I'll be right back. (*DUFF exits out the restroom door. <u>KNOCK</u> on the front door.*)

RON: Yeah?

IRENE'S VOICE: Ronnie? (*IRENE enters. She is covered with snow and has a red face. She takes off the snow and wipes the red off.*)

RON: Irene, what are you doing out here?

IRENE: I did it, Ronnie, I sold a painting.

RON: Hey, did you hear that, Junior? Irene sold a painting. I told you she was good.

JUNIOR: Nicely done, Irene.

RON: Which one?

IRENE: The wood ducks.

RON: Oh yeah, that's a good one.

IRENE: Oh, Ronnie, I'm so excited.

RON: Me, too. We gotta celebrate. Get out a coupla cold ones, Junior. My wife just sold a painting. What'd you get for it, honey?

IRENE: $20,000.

RON: What?

IRENE: $20,000. It's gonna be made into a stamp!

JUNIOR: A duck stamp? You gotta duck stamp?

IRENE: And if it goes national, I'll make five times that.

JUNIOR: You're famous, Irene.

IRENE: Let's all go out to Red Lobster, my treat.

JUNIOR: YOOOOO, Red Lobster.

RON: $20,000.

IRENE: I owe it all to you, Ronnie. First you shot them ducks. And then you got me to stuff 'em, and I gotta admit, I hated every minute of it. But by the time I started painting 'em, I don't mean to brag or nothing, but there wasn't much about a duck I didn't know, inside or out.

JUNIOR: Irene, if you want, I'll set you up a corner in the bait store, a gallery. I can even maybe even get you a guest spot painting on . . .

IRENE: I don't know about TV, Junior.

JUNIOR: I was gonna say the radio, but painting on TV might even be better.

RON: $20,000.

IRENE: Ron, I was so worried with the resort going under. I could see the toll it was takin' on you, but now we can afford to get out from under it, move into town if we want.

RON: Yeah . . .

DUFF: I warned you, Ron.

IRENE: This is just the beginning, too. Once you get a stamp you can sell 'em as fast as you can paint 'em.

JUNIOR: That's a fact. You'll never have to work again, Ronnie.

DUFF: I told you she was special, but you didn't listen.

RON: What are you saying, Duff? *(There's POUNDING on the door.)*

VOICE OF FRANCIS: Brother Ron, Brother Ron!

RON: Yeah, come on in, fellas. *(FRANCIS and SHUMWAY enter.)*

FRANCIS: Thank God you're still here. The end of the world is not at hand.

JUNIOR: Hey, I think you got something here.

FRANCIS: The judgment day is a long way off.

RON: How 'bout that? Perfect timing.

SHUMWAY: Brother Ron, I can breathe through my nose.

FRANCIS: It's a miracle.

SHUMWAY: Hashanah, hosanna, heavenly host, hosanna.

RON: That's hypothermia breathing for you, kid.

SHUMWAY: It feels wonderful. Naughty Nancy, nature's nymph numbly nestles Ned.

FRANCIS: A miracle.

JUNIOR: Ronnie, your bobber's going under.

RON: All right.

SHUMWAY: Mighty Maurice, man of men, meticulously masturbates mice.

FRANCIS: Saint Shumway.

RON: Now what are you doing, Irene?

IRENE: Ron, I'm painting the ceiling like the Sistine Chapel, only Adam is gonna be a walleye and God's finger is a Johnson cast master.

JUNIOR: Ron, your bobber.

DUFF: I warned you, Ronnie.

RON: What?

DUFF: You two are set for life.

RON: You're right there, Duffer, yoooooo.

DUFF: Like Junior's dog.

RON: Duff, Irene's not gonna jump in no lake without her sweater.

DUFF: Not Irene—I'm talking about you, Ron. I told you she was special, remember? But you didn't listen.

FRANCIS: We're saved.

DUFF: You're sunk. Next thing you know . . .

IRENE: She'll be finishing your sentences for you.

RON: Stop it, Duff. This . . .

IRENE: Ain't you talking, Ron. For one thing, I don't look like this.

RON AND IRENE: I haven't for years.

RON: It's how I remember you.

IRENE: And your brother, look at him.

BOTH: He died when he was twenty-five.

RON: He's my older brother, always will be.

DUFF: You gotta get him, Ronnie, for all of us.

RON: Duffer.

JUNIOR: Ron, your bobber, set the hook.

IRENE: Ron, we can move into town if we want.

RON: No, Irene, I don't want that in here.

IRENE: But I'm over half done.

RON: No. Irene, this is my place where I can go and be alone and think and if I want to remember you like this, I can, and my brother, I can, and Junior, and even these two nuts, I can . . .

IRENE: You want to be alone?

RON: Yes.

IRENE: If I leave, Ron, I'm not coming back here.

RON: Good, go.

IRENE: But.

RON: I don't want your goddamn painting, none of it.

(ICE CRACKS.)

JUNIOR: Hey, Ron.

RON: Hey, Junior, pull up a chair.

JUNIOR: Naw, thanks; once I set my ass down I never wanna get up, and Cookie's waiting for me. I just stopped out to see how you're doing.

RON: Fine.

JUNIOR: Sorry to hear about Irene.

RON: Yeah, thanks.

JUNIOR: She was something, boy.

RON: Yeah, she was.

JUNIOR: You know, me and Cookie are trying out a new restaurant in town, if you wanna go?

RON: No. Thanks, though.

JUNIOR: We've been doing that. Went to one the other day, "Peace Meal" it's called. I look on the menu—where's the four basic meat groups? And then you gotta ask for white bread. I got a plate of one of the terrible T's. I can't remember—tofu, tamari, tahini, tabouli, something. Washed it down with the swallows of cappuccino and, look, I got nothing against vegetarians, some of my favorite foodstuffs are vegetarians, but I left hungrier than when I walked in. Cut my mouth on my coffee cup that had a sculpture of an endangered species on the rim of the mug: sea urchin got me. Made me hope the damn things do go extinct so they don't put 'em on the coffee mugs. No offense to Irene, but the artists ruined everything.

RON: You can't say that, Junior.

JUNIOR: Used to be there was no such thing as art. If there was a drawing it was to say how to kill something . . . or a song was to bring rain. People use to know why they beat on drums; now you get these nincompoops coming up from the Cities with a new shirt and a twenty-dollar bill, and they don't change either. Beat some drums in the woods for a week, don't even know why. Go home. Have sex with their wives till they forget how, and have to wait another year to come up here again. And it was the goddamn artists come up here and turned us all into metaphors. Once you're a metaphor, you can't do nothing without it meaning something. I got to hand it to Irene, though: she seen it coming. Was smarter than the rest of us.

RON: I think she just liked to paint, Junior.

JUNIOR: She turned your perfectly good resort into an artist colony.

RON: You know as well as I do there were no more fish to catch. That's what saved the place. And I gotta admit, the bar never did better. I'd put an artist down on his luck up against a thirsty fisherman any day of the week.

JUNIOR: Well, all's I got to say is things have a habit of turning around. Coupla years ago I'm driving down Highway 7, having a hell of a bad day, when all of a sudden there's a chainsaw laying there in a box all oiled up and ready to go.

RON: Duffer, oh no.

JUNIOR: Good old Duffer. There was a man who knew his way around a chainsaw.

RON: I know; that's right. He'd go off in the woods and we wouldn't see him for days, and then he'd come home exhausted and out of gas. Not say a word. And then a story would come back how a hunter had got himself lost back in the woods somewhere he swore had never been seen by another human eye, about to give up hope, when there carved out of a tree was the image of a Viking or a pirate or Alfred E. Newman.

JUNIOR: Now, see, that's the kind of art I can relate to. I hate to say it, because of how much he pissed me off, but I really miss Duffer.

RON: Yeah, I miss you too, Junior.

JUNIOR: Shut up.

RON: I do.

JUNIOR: Well, don't tell me.

RON: How did you go, Junior?

JUNIOR: Heart attack, can you believe it?

RON: Same as Irene.

JUNIOR: Yeah. Look, I gotta get moving, Ronnie.

RON: All right, Junior.

JUNIOR: Good luck.

RON: What?

JUNIOR: With the hog.

RON: Oh yeah. Think he's down there?

JUNIOR: It's my job to think so. Later.

RON: Later. *(JUNIOR exits. LIGHTS up on IRENE.)*

IRENE: Hey, Ronnie.

RON: Hey, Irene. How long you been there?

IRENE: The whole time.

RON: I'm sorry, Irene. Hey, I just got the new brochure from that art colony you went to. You're in there with the cartoon man and the mountain painter.

IRENE: Oh yeah? Which painting did they pick?

RON: They got your mallards. Boy, they look good enough to shoot.

IRENE: How's Darlene?

RON: She's down in the Cities now, happy as can be. We talk every coupla weeks. She comes up for holidays. She's going into fashion.

IRENE: Fashion.

RON: She's special, Irene.

IRENE: Yeah, I'm afraid she is. We used to have to scotch-tape bows to her head.

RON: Still do, you should see her new haircut. It's a different world out there, Irene. We were kids and the family would go down to the Cities for shopping or whatnot and on the way home we'd stop and get a coupla burgers. Dad yells, "Clean up the car kids." And we'd get all the wrappers and cups and whatever else was on the floor and hand it up to the old man and, zing, out the window with it. Then we'd quick look out the back to watch it hit and explode.

"There's my Coke cup, there's my french fries." "Hey, goddammit," Dad yells. "Who put the bottle in there? Now my case is gonna be one short!" And we'd giggle, flying up Highway 7 at eighty-five miles an hour past the farms. All of a sudden my dad says, "Watch this kids, magic." All the lights went out in all the farmhouses like a power outage, and Dad says, "Ten o'clock," without even looking at his watch. I thought he was the Amazing Kreskin, when in fact he knew Cronkite had just finished the news and all the farmers were off to bed. We all had the same heartbeat then. Now it seems crazy.

IRENE: Why did you come out here, Ron?

RON: I wanted to find you.

IRENE: How did you know I'd be out here?

RON: Now don't get upset, Irene, but this was the one place I told you never to go.

IRENE: Well, I'm going to bed. Ronnie, you coming up?

RON: Yeah, I'll be up there in a minute. *(IRENE exits. YOUNG RON HUBER enters the icehouse.)*

YOUNG RON: Hey.

RON: Hey.

YOUNG RON: Any luck?

RON: No.

YOUNG RON: What are you after?

RON: A monster that lives down there.

YOUNG RON: Oh.

RON: Well, what do you know for sure?

YOUNG RON: I know your stove ain't on. And you sank your truck, but it was a Chevy, anyhow. I know when I grow up I'm gonna catch the biggest fish in this lake. Me and my brother. And I'll get a place on this lake and run it. No girls allowed except one, and I'm going to marry her. She's special, but I don't mind. In fact, I like it.

RON: You do, huh?

YOUNG RON: Yeah, I like it a lot.

TIM: So much for the Storm of the Century. Kind of petered out. I swore we were in for one there at first . . . I'm afraid tomorrow it's a beautiful day. So here's the schools that are open. Class will resume at Frazee, private and parochial; Fridley, private and parochial; Fulda, private and parochial; Gary, private and parochial; Glencoe, private and parochial.

End of Play

TIM: *(Continues, fading out.)* Glenville Edmonds, private and parochial; Goodhue, private and parochial; Goodridge, private and parochial; Grand Meadow, private and parochial; Grand Rapids, private and parochial; Granite Falls–Clarkfield; private and parochial; Greenbush, private and parochial; Greenway-Colleraine, private and parochial; Grey Eagle, private and parochial; Grygla-Gatzke, private and parochial . . .

TAKING NAMES

FROM *OF MIRTH AND MISCHIEF*

No man wakes knowing who he is. That's the first thing I do every morning: I check. *Oh, it's me.*

But now, I don't know who I am. Yesterday a man came to the door. My mom said he was a census taker. I asked, "What's a census taker?" She said, "He came and he took our names."

I cried because I liked my name, and now a strange man has taken it.

If that wasn't bad enough, Mom told me that in the hole in the wall where we plug in the lamp, *there lives a bumble bee, leave him alone or he'll sting me.* I don't think we should have a bee in the wall, so I get a butter knife and go digging for him. He got me anyway. I fly across the room, and now there's a big black mark on the wall and we have to plug the lamp into another socket.

I have a sister and a brother. My sister is mostly kind to me. She invites me to tea parties and she tries out haircuts on me before she gives them to her dolls. I don't fight much with her because I learned early, brothers fight for many reasons, but sisters fight to win.

My brother is a work in progress. First of all, he can't talk. I do all the talking for him. He's always hungry. People think he has anger issues because he walks around with two fists. What they don't know is his hands are holding donuts. He's afraid of the lights that move across the wall of our room at night. They are made by passing cars, but he doesn't know that. Mom sings to him a song called "Nighty-Night to Brother," and he calms down.

It's nighty-night to brother, to brother, to brother,
It's nighty-night to brother, 'cause we all love him so.

I tell Mom I see things, too, in the corners of my eye, or hear sounds. She says it's only my imagination. *Oh no,* I think, *now it could be anything!*

But I go to sleep with the muffled sound of my parents talking and laughing. There's no better way to fall asleep. I feel safe.

In the morning, we get in the car. Just me and Mom and Dad. I am the chosen one, my brother and sister have to stay home. The man must have brought my name back in the night, because my mom calls me Kevin. Dad is next to me. His white cotton shirt smells like Pall Mall cigarettes. Mom sits on the other side and sings.

We drive for two hours, and then we turn into a very large parking lot.

Now I remember—I'm going to the hospital today. Shriners Hospital for Crippled Children. Shriners are very good men. Their main transportation is go-carts shaped like helicopters. When we talked about this, my parents made it sound better than the zoo.

However, Mom keeps crying, and Dad tells me to be a man. Being a man is never good.

I'm relieved to see the face of good old Dr. Tippy in the lobby.

And we're standing there in the lobby when Mom turns away. Then Dad helps her to the front door. Dr. Tippy says, "It's alright, Kevin, it's alright."

When an adult says it's alright, you know it is not alright.

They take x-rays, which are pictures you don't have to smile for. Dr. Tippy takes me into a room and looks at my arm. He tries to uncurl my left arm. *Ouch!* He asks if I can squeeze his finger. Now *he* says ouch.

A man writes as Dr. Tippy says, "Absent radius, thrombosis, blood flow, ligament, platelets." He seems happy, I already know when a doctor is happy, it isn't necessarily a good thing. Then he brings me into a room with children with missing pieces. That's when it hits me.

This is a drop-off center for children with missing pieces.

He puts me in a baby bed. A baby bed! I had a real-boy bed at home, with a Roy Rogers blanket, and now he's jamming me in a baby bed!

That night I look out the window. I see a crow calling into the night. I see the moon.

Before I even know it, I start singing. "Nighty-Night to Brother."

*   *   *

The next day Grandmother visits. I tell her about the census man taking my name. She said when she was a girl in the Ozark mountains, a census man came to her cabin once. She thought he was a revenuer, so she met him with a shotgun. He said, "No, no, I'm a census taker."

She didn't know what that was.

He said he was trying to find out how many people live in the United States.

Grandma says, "I told him he come to the wrong house. I got no idea."

She has sayings like, "Boy, you're as mixed up as a dog's lunch." Or she tells me, "Boy, don't let 'em beat the meanness out of you."

I love my grandmother. We seem to be in the same place in terms of reality, in the same light: me at dawn, she at dusk, both of us on the hazy borders between the known, the unknown, and unknowable.

There's one big difference. While I can still see the spirits, she has names for them. Elves and fairies, the wee people, she calls them. Leave out a plate of food at night, or they'll do you mischief.

"You do that, too, Grandma. I've seen you."

"Shhhh . . . don't upset them." She tells me they love green and red. Sunlight kills them. There's the Aswang, from the Philippines, with a long snout. He'll suck your blood if you don't clean your room. There's the Mugliwump from Australia, a sea monster that takes greedy children. Tiny trolls that lived in teeth, if you don't brush them out. Belly button trolls that have lint mines. Changelings that switch places with human babies at birth. You can catch a changeling because baby elves can talk, so you fry egg shells in a pan, then they'll ask, "Why are you doing that, why are you frying egg shells?" and you have them.

Before I knew Grandma, there were two types of fairytales: ones I didn't like, and ones I hadn't heard yet. I hated fairytales. Guys like me always got a bad deal. Snow White trades in seven perfectly good little guys for one big one.

But Grandma's stories are different. Grandma says stories are medicine, they can heal or destroy. Or, a story must be told at its proper time. Or, a good story helps us know how we belong. Or, whenever you tell a story you've heard, the person you heard it from will be on your right shoulder. And the person they heard it from on their shoulder all the way back to the first. If you lose your way, look up and to the right, I'll be there.

Thanks, Grandmother.

BIRD OPERA

FROM *FLIGHT*

Crow

Crow, son of a crow—
on the crime scene, in the know,
all dressed up in graveyard black,
fingerprints behind his back—
crow, son of a crow.

Crow, fly away from here,
fly away, my fear!
Crow, fly away from here,
fly away, my fear!

Two upon the fence,
then three to pick the evidence.
A flock of cousins take their stations,
estimations, accusations.
Another sector, 'nother call:
one flies, then two, then all,
over rivers, fields, and cities,
administrations and committees.
Up and over roads they rise, and

off into the gray horizon,
afraid to be the last who goes.
Crows, no crows.

Crow, fly away from here—
Fly away, my fear!
Crow, fly away from here—
Fly away, my fear!

Hummingbird

Hummingbird, hummingbird,
not a word, not a word,
d'Artagnan of the summer yard,
petite amour, ooh la, en garde,
tasting the queen's tangerines,
beneath flora's finest seen.
Oh, you delicate gent,
with tiny foil, heaven sent,
heartbeats pour like a rolling drum,
play your cadence, with a hummmmmmm—
then, up and away to the next kingdom.

Rooster

Rooster, rooster!
Was it you that caused the hens to stir?
Is that dried blood on your spur?
What does your crying say?
Do you announce the new day
or boast the end of amorous nights?
Take a rest, try to relax.
The man with the ax,
like you, has appetites.

Woodpecker

Woodpecker
woodpecker woodpecker woodpecker woodpecker
woodpecker woodpecker—
that knocking makes my head explode!
Perhaps if I could break your code,
I would anxiously await tomorrow's episode.

Woodpecker woodpecker,
who is on the other line?
What secrets do you hammer home?
Can't you whisper,
can't you pray?
Is this the way, is this the divine way,
is this the way you pray?

Canada Goose

He still makes the trip twice a year,
past sights once shared by two.
The memories
make him cry out, as
each place reminds him of you.

He makes the trip twice a year,
and carries, where once held joy,
the emptiness
that sends him to
look for love among the decoys.

Canada goose, keep soaring,
take your song high off the ground.
How could emptiness be so heavy?
Don't let your heavy heart drag you down.

Blackbird

With his bright orange epaulettes,
Marsh Marshall, Marsh Marshall,
on the cattail bravely sits.
blackbird orders in the day.

Let the frog hold down the bottom,
take your song to the sun,
let the swamp dry up in autumn,
lead the way.

The chorus last all summer long.

You can have your piney forest,
don't need no deep blue sea,
give me a swamp thing any time
for soniferous shindiggery.

So listen for the call
on the far side of the corn
shouting orders in falsetto.

Man, that bird looks good in a uniform.

Hawk

This is where I was going,
this is fine, set me down.

I didn't even hear you.
Where did you come from?
You never made a sound.
I really appreciate this ride.

Is that your home?
I hear children inside.

All right, we'll stop for a minute, but really, you must know,
I have obligations.
It's been lovely, the missus likes to worry,
please let me go!

Sparrow

See here, sparrow,
you were brought here from Europe
to clean horse manure from the streets.
There were *jobs* when you first arrived.
Your large families kept our streets clean,
you were brought here and thrived.

Now there aren't any horses,
your color is dull,
your song is a sin,
your nests are filthy,
your women resemble the men.
You're not from here anyway.
Go back, or away,

I love my song,
another life,
our family's large,
I love my wife.
I am sad you feel this way,
but we are here
and here we'll stay.

Nighthawks

Tonight, the drive-in movie has a double feature.
Dad adjusts the window speaker,
teenagers pour from an open trunk door
like a clown car.
An animated elephant says, three minutes more
they close the snack bar.
On-screen coming attractions
become visible in the twilight.
Then come the nighthawks, aerial action,
mosquito dogfight.
As a lawn tractor passes, pulling a compressor billowing smoke, we see
my sister and her friends dance behind it like magic fairies in the mists of
    DDT.

A Chorus of Birds

A pew of cardinals.
A cord of wood ducks.
A pentagon of hawks.
A penitentiary of pigeons.
A traffic jam of geese.
An asylum of loons.
A Versace of peacocks.
A jury of blue jays.
An Advil of woodpeckers.
A co-op of doves.
A waiting room of storks.
A flinching of ducks.

Kling and Simone Perrin premiered "How? How? Why? Why? Why?" at the Seattle Repertory Theatre in 2008. (CHRIS BENNION)

The trumpet is a trickster at "How? How? Why? Why? Why?" (CHRIS BENNION)

Back Home with Mason Jennings at the Fitzgerald Theater, 2012. (TOM CAMPBELL)

The house band for *Of Mirth and Mischief* included, from left, Dietrich Poppen (obscured, kneeling), Steve Kramer, Noah Smith, James Diers, Aaron Clarksean, Bill Shaw, Jacob Hanson, Marc Anderson, Haley Bonar. (TOM CAMPBELL)

Kling and Steve Kramer in the infamous elves photo shoot for *Of Mirth and Mischief*, 2011. (ANN MARSDEN)

Kling and Steve Kramer prepare for *Of Mirth and Mischief*. (ANN MARSDEN)

Three views from *Back Home* with Mason Jennings at the Fitzgerald Theater, 2012. (TOM CAMPBELL)

Scarecrow on Fire: The Lost Notebooks of Oz at the Fitzgerald Theater, 2010. (TOM CAMPBELL)

SCARECROW ON FIRE: The Lost Notebooks of Oz

Cast

SCARECROW, DOCTOR'S ASSISTANT

DOROTHY

TIN MAN, NURSE

LION, LAB TECH

DRY GOODS MAN

NEWSPAPER MAN

WIZARD, DOCTOR

GUY

TOTO TWO

MAN

TIN MAN *may also play roles of* NEWSPAPER MAN *and* TOTO TWO

LION *may also play roles of* DRY GOODS MAN, GUY, MAN, WIZARD, *and* DOCTOR

Act I

Song: "If I Only Had a Brain"

SCARECROW: Something wasn't quite right with the land of Oz. Years had passed since Dorothy, the girl from Kansas, had arrived, killed both wicked witches, then left for Kansas. On that very same day, the Wizard of Oz had blown away in his balloon, leaving Glinda, the Witch of the North, the only one left with magic, and it was all good. Every day was beautiful, it only rained when we needed it, and even then it was gumdrops and jellybeans. There was peace. All the time. The Lion was now King of the Beasts; I rarely saw him, but it was said that he grew fat and lazy in his lair, sat in a recliner looking up at his framed medal of bravery. The Tin Man now ruled the Land of the Winkies, and he lived in the castle that the Wicked Witch used to live in. Most of it was a museum now, with her crystal ball and cauldron in a section called "Off Limits." They said the Tin Man sighed a lot, remembering lost loves. Now that everyone loved everyone, he pined for the intensity of a love that could go wrong.

My brain softened as well. I did crossword puzzles and invented ground-breaking theorems, but what good were they compared to magic? Often I felt as bored as I felt back on a post in the cornfield again. I missed my crows. They're actually amazing creatures. They aren't evil, like others believe. They're simply messengers, and they take away things we don't want. Really, if you have a problem give it to a crow; they'll fly away with it. I went to my old cornfield and found a crow. I asked him if he can take problems away, can he bring one back? "Of course," he said and was off. A short time later he returned. "Well?" I asked. Here is what he said: "Only a fool does not plan for trouble in times of peace." What does that mean? I need more. He was gone. When he returned he said, "A healthy mind is a curious mind and a curious mind needs to master that which makes it curious." Weird. He flew away, taking with him some concerns I had about a recent election.

I went back to Oz but couldn't forget what the crow had said. This is when I did something. Something against all the rules, but I had to know. Was Oz in danger? "Prepare for trouble in times of peace." That's what he'd said. I did what I thought best. I went to the Wicked Witch's castle. No sign of the Tin Man. I heard a buffer wheel whizzing in another room and a long "AHHH, that's it," so I went to her study and found her magic crystal ball. The memories flooded back: the great battles, the fire. I walked up to the ball . . . I peered in. The girl, Dorothy. She was holding her head, screaming.

(FIRST VIDEO of Dorothy emerges.)

DOROTHY: Help! Please! Scarecrow on fire, Scarecrow on fire! You have to help!

SCARECROW: Dorothy, it's me, Scarecrow. Dorothy. Come back!

Suddenly I heard a voice from the other room.

TIN MAN: Who is that? Who is there? The museum is closed.

SCARECROW: I think it was the Tin Man himself. Then a sound like a box of empty cans dropping down the stairs. And then,

TIN MAN: Ouch. That'll leave a dent.

SCARECROW: I snuck away, careful not to leave any straw behind. What had Dorothy said? "Scarecrow on fire?" That's impossible. Fire was against the law in Oz. Too dangerous. So was water, for the same reason. What was the matter with Dorothy? She was clearly in distress. This question was larger than mere brains. It would take heart and courage. Needless to say, the next day I sent forth a call to action. Two flying monkeys were dispatched to the jungle and Winkie country, and quick as a hiccup, the Lion and Tin Man stood in my chambers.

The Tin Man was polished and buffed to where his metal must have been thin as foil, and the Lion had developed a bit of a paunch and wore a horrible, pungent, eye-watering cologne, a flavor he called "Snarl," which he proudly stated he had invented himself. He certainly had not lost his courage, for it took a great deal to wear that stench. I greeted my friends. We embraced. I wondered about my own appearance. Had I aged as they had? The Lion did say he missed my old face. As the new wizard, I could afford any artist in the country to paint my face and of course chose the very best. However, this meant I was often subjected to whatever style was in vogue. Naturalism suited me best; unfortunately, a wave of the avant-garde was rolling through at the time and consequently words and numbers adorned my cheek and brow with sentences bashing the status quo, "Bring Down the Man," which ironically was me. But we do support the arts in Oz.

Anyhow . . . I turned to my comrades and said, "I wish this were a social visit. We're long overdue, but I'm afraid we have work to do." They immediately picked up on the seriousness of the matter.

The Lion spoke first.

LION: You just tell me what to kill, I'll kill it.

SCARECROW: The Tin Man chimed in as well.

TIN MAN: My heart is with you, one hundred percent.

SCARECROW: My friends, I knew I could count on you. All right, listen. Dorothy is in trouble.

The Tin Man repeated,

TIN MAN: Dor-o-thy?

SCARECROW: Why did he pronounce her name like that? Drove me crazy. The second "o" is obviously silent.

Yes, Dorothy. I saw it in the crystal ball.

TIN MAN: But that's . . .

SCARECROW: I know. Forbidden.

TIN MAN: That was YOU in my castle.

SCARECROW: Yes, but I saw Dorothy, and she is in trouble. We must go to Kansas. Look, we still have the ruby slippers. They are like a door to other worlds, but—like a door—they remain here in Oz. I say we don the ruby slippers one at a time, go to Kansas, find Dorothy, catch a quick tornado, and the four of us will be back before we're even missed.

The Lion was aboard immediately.

LION: I'm in.

SCARECROW: Not so much the Tin Man.

TIN MAN: But remember you once said . . .

SCARECROW: Forget what I once said.

TIN MAN: All right, I'm in.

SCARECROW: The next week we assembled in the Munchkin town square. It was early. All the flowers were closed tight. I told the others,

I'll go first. Then I'll wait for you in Kansas. Lion, you come next.

LION: All right. Good luck.

SCARECROW: The Tin Man started to cry.

TIN MAN: I always liked you best.

SCARECROW: I'll see you in five minutes.

Suddenly the Lion yelled,

LION: Oh, no! Look! It's Glinda!

SCARECROW: Sure enough, the telltale floating bubble that Glinda, the Witch of the North, liked to ride around in, was bearing down upon us. The Tin Man lost it.

TIN MAN: We are dead.

SCARECROW: The Lion roared.

LION: Go. Go! We'll hold her off. Just go get Dorothy.

SCARECROW: As fast as I could, I stuffed the straw from my feet into the ruby slippers and said, "I want to be in Kansas." Nothing happened.

TIN MAN: You have to tap the heels, remember?

SCARECROW: I tapped the heels three times, and as Glinda's face emerged from the bubble, I began to lose focus. And then, and then, the world began to spin, my head, my body a blur. It was as if I was being summoned and then, there it was! It was glorious. It was . . . Kansas.

Song: "Home Sweet Home" (with video)

SCARECROW: I landed hard in a field. I got up and surveyed my surroundings. Gray. It was so gray. The rain was wet and tasted nothing of gumdrops. I walked along a most unyellow brick road, every once in a while passing human people like Dorothy. Some greeted me, others saw my cloth-wrapped head and wondered if I was infectious. "We have no disease in Oz," I proudly stated. I take that back. There was an outbreak of giddiness once in Munchkin Land, but that ran through pretty fast and was actually quite pleasant. I laughed at the memory. They covered their mouths and ran away.

As I made my way, I thought of Oz. I found it so different than Kansas. I have to say the scarecrows here are just plain idiots. I tried several times to strike up a conversation. They just sit there. And the trees . . . nothing. Are they stuck up, or what? I couldn't even get a rise out of an oak. Then I thought, even in Oz it had been a long while since trees verbally abused me, let alone threw an apple. And I remembered when every flower used to hatch a Munchkin. Now you'll be lucky to find one in every four and always a perennial. It's all coroners and lollipop suckers. Were we becoming Kansas? It rained for days. In Oz, a storm meant impending evil, but here, it's just gray gloom.

I became more amazed by people that lived in Kansas. All this gray. How wonderfully subtle their palates must be. No wonder Dorothy found the color of Oz so overwhelming. Maybe it's that in Oz all the color is on the outside and the black and white is on the inside, and in Kansas it's quite the opposite. My spirits were dropping. My straw was molding. Then one day the sun came out. I saw fields of green. It was beautiful. New life sprouting all around. A green that held in it every color of the rainbow. That's how they did it in Kansas. One color at a time, but they sure do it right.

I entered a dry goods store. Men sat about drinking coffee, chatting. One man sat behind a counter. He kept licking the end of a pencil. Writing something down. Then saying,

DRY GOODS MAN: That ain't right.

SCARECROW: Licking the eraser. Then rubbing it briskly.

DRY GOODS MAN: Whoops, now I done it. Dad burn it.

SCARECROW: He looked up from the page.

DRY GOODS MAN: Feller who done my books was a crook. Goes to show figures don't lie, but a liar can figure.

SCARECROW: Other men said,

GUY: That bookkeeping feller weren't no good. From the city.

NEWSPAPER MAN: Are you from the city?

SCARECROW: No, I was born in a cornfield.

They liked that.

DRY GOODS MAN: Is the bag on your head covering a accident?

NEWSPAPER MAN: Is you a vet?

SCARECROW: I said,

No, the bag keeps the straw in.

They thought this was funny. One man was staring at a large paper, the *Wichita Times*. We have no written language in Oz. All of our proclamations are blank, and the officials hold them up for show and say a speech. The man never looked up from the paper. I felt bad for him, poor man obviously infected with the alphabet. Then he did the most amazing thing, he got up and changed the time on the clock. Moved it ahead an hour. We don't have time in Oz either. Time doesn't matter because no one ever ages. If you're a child, you're always a child. Time never moves forward or back. I know about time from Dorothy, and I am amazed this man can change time by reading a newspaper. Is he a wizard? He says,

NEWSPAPER MAN: No. I just read today is daylight savings time.

SCARECROW: That must be the name of the spell. Then I realized that it had taken the hour from my life. I was angry. That was an hour I could've spent in search of Dorothy. I demanded that he put the hour back.

NEWSPAPER MAN: Can't do that. Hey, my show is on.

SCARECROW: Another man turned a knob on a box, and a voice emerged. Was there a little man in there, a Munchkin?

NEWSPAPER MAN: No, it's a radio. Ain't you ever seen a radio?

SCARECROW: Is it a crystal ball?

NEWSPAPER MAN: Naw, it works on invisible waves.

SCARECROW: Sounds like a crystal ball to me.

The voice on the radio was saying,

WIZARD: Brothers and sisters, Power Pill side effects may include a sudden rise in self-esteem, temporary loss of inhibitions, a spreading rash of success, reoccurring respectability, increasing inflammation of ego, irregardless of ir-ritating irregularities, vicarious visits and ventings vesuvulating from various vixens, a burning sensation to touch, may lift the hem of prosperity and gaze through gates hitherto closed, outbursts of "eureka" and "oh yes, oh yes oh yes!" If you've got the will, I got the pill. Gotta stuck throttle, I got the bottle. If the effects last more than four hours call your doctor, call your priest, you're gonna wanna call everybody. Tell 'em to get on down to the intersection of RR 2 and double D . . . look for the blinking red light of the WOOZ tower. The blinking beacon of truth. Follow instructions on label. Results may vary.

SCARECROW: That voice—it sounded familiar. I know it! That was the Wizard—the Wizard of Oz. Then something remarkable happened.

WIZARD: Well, now we have a special treat. A song by Miss Dorothy Gale. Hello, Miss Gale.

DOROTHY: Hello, Wizard.

WIZARD: How old are you, Miss Gale?

DOROTHY: I'm sixteen.

WIZARD: Sixteen years old.

DOROTHY: Almost.

WIZARD: I see. So how did you come to enter the Little Miss Western Kansas Beauty Pageant?

DOROTHY: Well, my Auntie Em, she's my aunt that I live with, she said, "Dorothy, honey, beauty is a tool like a crowbar, and I want you to use it to pry yourself from this godforsaken existence."

WIZARD: I see.

DOROTHY: She said other things too.

WIZARD: She did, did she?

DOROTHY: Yes. "Get out fast. Boys around here are dumber than the dirt under their fingernails."

WIZARD: Anything else?

DOROTHY: Uh huh. "What happens in Kansas leaves Kansas."

WIZARD: Why don't we get to your talent. Now this is the song you sang for the talent portion.

DOROTHY: That's right.

WIZARD: And what happened?

DOROTHY: What?

WIZARD: You won!

DOROTHY: Yes, yes I did.

WIZARD: Where did you learn this song?

DOROTHY: Remember the tornado last April that swept through?

WIZARD: I think we all remember that.

DOROTHY: Well, my dog bit the neighbor, an old witch.

WIZARD: You don't mean that.

DOROTHY: I do, she was going to take Toto.

WIZARD: Toto?

DOROTHY: My dog. So I ran away. That's where I met you. Remember?

WIZARD: I do remember. I was selling . . . medicine . . . from my . . . Then what happened?

DOROTHY: I came back home and hit my head and went to a land called Oz and a scarecrow taught it to me.

WIZARD: Well, Miss Gale, you are certainly interesting.

DOROTHY: I changed it a bit for the pageant.

WIZARD: I see. Brothers and sisters. Dorothy Gale singing her rendition of "If I Only Had a Brain" from her talent portion of the Little Miss Western Kansas Beauty Pageant.

Song: "If I Only Had a Brain"

DOROTHY: *(Sings the familiar lyrics, ending with:)*

I would free all the hostages,

Feed the nations,

Cure all diseases that cause pain.

I'd adopt all the homeless children,

Bring peace and love to all mankind, if I only had a brain.

SCARECROW: I know her! That's Dorothy. I need to find her.

The dry goods man said he knew her as well.

DRY GOODS MAN: Yeah. That's Dorothy Gale.

SCARECROW: The man looked up from the paper.

NEWSPAPER MAN: She lives just down this road a piece.

SCARECROW: Thank you, thank you all.

And as fast as straw can fly, I was out the door.

Song: "I'm Going Down" (with video)

LION: Is this thing on? Is this thing on?

Being a lion, I don't fear anything, but Glinda was pretty upset. I guess, well, obviously someone can be good and still get upset. She was all, "You fools—you know not what you have wrought! You are never, never meant to travel to that world, you'll upset the balance, the delicate balance!" The Tin Man was sniveling, and I was all, "Put 'em up, put 'em up, put 'em up." Finally Glinda said, "All right, just go. Find the Scarecrow and come back here as fast as you can. You'll find out soon enough you have no business there. Fools!" I could hear her still ranting in the bubble as it faded away. "Men. Can't live with 'em . . . "

I took the slippers. Crammed the end of my paws in them, clicked my heels, and *pow*. There I was in what I guess was Kansas. Wherever I was, the Scarecrow was nowhere in sight. But there were plenty of people like Dorothy and the Wizard. All staring at me. And pointing. I checked my beard for crumbs. That wasn't it. I said, "I need to find Dorothy." It's like they'd never seen a lion before. I tried to smile, but it only made them step back and gasp. I heard one clearly state, "And that smell." It's called "Snarl," I said, but the word sounded more like an example of itself. In fact, every time I tried to speak the sound came out low and gravely. It seemed I had command of absolutely no consonants.

One man wondered if I was from Yerp. "You smell fruity, like a Yerpean." Now, I can sense fear. It was low level at this point but building rapidly. "He is," said another, "a dad burn Yerpean from Yerp." I tried to explain, and in an attempt to put them at ease I dropped from an upright stance to all fours. That's when someone yelled, "That ain't no Yerpean from Yerp—it's a lion! AHHHHH." Suddenly everyone was running in terror. Well, of course I was a lion. I was a lion five minutes ago. What had changed? Nothing. Perception, that's all. That's when I realized that people in Kansas don't believe what they see—rather, they see what they believe.

In a short time they were joined by others dressed a bit like the Wizard's guards, all pointing sticks at me. A net was thrown over me. I have three roars I use on occasion. One is the basic "back off" roar. You know, "You're in my space." Then there's the roar I call "territorial"—meant to defend an area. More of a "Hey you—get off my lawn." It's a bit more aggressive. Then there's the full-blown knee weakener. The thing about this roar is you have to be prepared to back it up. It is not a threat, not an if/then scenario. That's more Scarecrowy. No, this roar is meant to say, "It's already too late . . ." ROAR. At which point a dart came from one of the sticks and, *whap,* into my hip. Faster than a field of poppies, I was out.

TIN MAN: The heart is a machine. A beautiful machine . . . if you listen, you can hear the mechanics at play. But it isn't a pump. No, the heart actually twists the blood out. The heart is a twister. There are but two emotions, fear and love: every other emotion is a subset of those two emotions. The Lion and I work like two sides of the coin, each trying not to let our emotions rule us. It's why we really need the common sense of Scarecrow . . . and each other.

I have to find my friends, now. I'm also in desperate need of a lube and polish. I came to a knee-high man standing beside the road. He stood quite still, pointing down the road to a garage. I'm guessing it's a kind of healing center for machines. I thanked the knee-high man and made my creaking way to the station. Next to the station was a dry goods store. I could hear men laughing inside. A man unfettered by hygiene asked me, "What are you doing in the lobby? Machines out back." Well, I never. I went "out back" to find a horrific display of disassembled autos, candy machines, implements. I ran back to the front of the building, shouting to the able-bodied cars, "Follow me! To the hills!!" Nothing. Their subservience so entrenched, they sat mute.

I decided to make my protests known back in the lobby when I spotted the most disgusting piece of trash sitting right out where everyone could see it. A picture book so loaded with filth it left nothing to the imagination. Wiring, diagrams, photographs of . . . parts. "Schematics," they were called, and I mean it showed everything. I shouted, "What if a toy were to roll in here and see this garbage?" The biggest offender, *Popular Mechanics*. Popular, I bet, and a host of self-proclaimed manuals loaded with pictorial "how to" sections that would put a sheen on a bulldozer. I have never felt like such an . . . object. I made my way back to the knee-high man, prepared to chastise him, when a man behind him stood up and asked,

GUY: Why are you talking to a fire hydrant?

TIN MAN: I was wondering if there is a place more, how should I put it, "civilized." I can't imagine Dorothy would tolerate a place such as this.

GUY: Yeah, yeah, there's Wichita.

TIN MAN: Wichita?

GUY: Yeah, it's a city.

TIN MAN: Is it a good Wichita or a bad Wichita?

GUY: Well, what's it like where you're from?

TIN MAN: "Oh," I said.

Oz is wonderful—full of love and beauty.

GUY: That is what you'll find in Wichita.

TIN MAN: I thanked my companion and his companion the fire hydrant. As I parted, I paused and asked him,

What if I would've said Oz was horrible, full of cutthroats and thieves?

GUY: I would've answered the same. That's what you'll find in Wichita. We find what we search for . . .

TIN MAN: Thank you, sir. You are the first thing that has made sense in Kansas.

And that is how I found myself on the road to Wichita and adventures beyond my wildest imagination.

Song: "Too Many Treasures" (with video)

SCARECROW: I probably weigh twenty pounds, and upon leaving the dry goods store down the gravel road the headwind every so often blew me back past the store. I came to a knee-high man and asked him which way to Dorothy Gale. Another man stood up from behind the knee-high man, looked at me, and said,

GUY: If this isn't the strangest day. If one more feller talks to that fire hydrant, I'm giving up the bottle.

SCARECROW: The man said the Gale farm was

GUY: That-a-way.

SCARECROW: I climbed in a trailer of hay bales. I nestled in. It was like a family reunion among all that hay. In fact, for a moment in all the laughter and singing, the weight of my mission was mercifully relieved. Finally I came to a farm. Everything about this farm was familiar. The water pump, the cellar door, the barn, the pigpen. I could've walked it with my eyes painted shut. Then I remembered this is the farm Dorothy described so well. I saw an older woman. It was Auntie Em. It must be. She fed the chickens, looked up at the sky, and went back inside. Auntie Em, the real Auntie Em, like seeing a god, a hero.

We have no gods in Oz. We have witches and wizards and talking pumpkins, but no one of the magnitude of Auntie Em. This trip was already worth whatever pain Glinda inflicted on my return. I had seen Auntie Em. Should I speak to her? What does one tell a god? Should I tell her my concerns? They say if you want to make gods laugh, tell them your plans. I decided to stay hidden until I knew the situation. So I plopped in the corner of the barn and waited. Dorothy would have to be here somewhere. It was home, after all.

At nightfall a dog was let outside. He barked and barked. There were no dogs in Oz. We had wolves, but no dogs. They really are a human invention. Toto for example, Dorothy's dog, was a terrier from the word *terra,* of the earth. His breed was designed over years to tirelessly work the ground for rodents. Toto Number One lived by three rules: everything he saw, he either ate it, dated it, or hated it. He also kept Dorothy grounded. This dog was the image of Toto. It took several days before he came close enough to where I could approach him.

Pssst. Toto. Toto. Psst. Toto, I know you can talk.

TOTO: Of course I can talk, and I'm not Toto. That's my dad. I'm his son, Toto Two.

SCARECROW: Toto Two?

TOTO: Toto Two.

SCARECROW: I'm the Scarecrow.

TOTO: I know who you are. My dad told me all about Oz . . . and you.

SCARECROW: Toto Two, I'm here looking for Dorothy.

TOTO: She's gone.

SCARECROW: Where?

TOTO: I don't know, but she left a while ago. It's just me and Aunt Em now.

SCARECROW: I have to find Dorothy, Toto. I think she's in trouble.

TOTO: Toto Two.

SCARECROW: Toto Two.

TOTO: Well, I shouldn't say this. She kept a diary.

SCARECROW: Go get it.

TOTO: You should never read a person's diary. Even I know that.

SCARECROW: Go get it, Toto Two.

TOTO: Okay, but it's not very interesting. Not much about me.

SCARECROW: You can read?

TOTO: "Though he be little, he be fierce." Shakespeare. Can I read . . .

SCARECROW: The little dog left and came back with a little book. While the dog was gone, I realized I was going to have to read. I was acquainted with the alphabet but refused to traffic in it for fear of being swayed by rhetoric. It's so emotional. No, stick to numbers, they don't let you down. But if it meant saving Dorothy, so be it.

TOTO: Turn to page fifty-three.

SCARECROW: I turned to page fifty-three. The diary read . . .

DOROTHY: Dear Diary, Uncle Henry isn't with us anymore. I will miss him. He had a thick accent from a place no one was allowed to talk about. Some say his family ran from a war, others say his family started the war. Henry wasn't talking. What is past is past, he would say. Even though he had a hard life and a face to hold a three-day rain, Em would say, he had a twinkle in his eye that betrayed a mischief looking for a way out.

Uncle Henry grew older. He became diabetic. He lost a leg. Whittled himself a new one out of a two-by-four. He continued to farm. For church he'd take the leg from under the corner of the dining room table. It was walnut, had been lathed with an ornate design. He'd prop up the table with his whittled leg until they got back from church. When he died, Aunt Em had him buried with that table leg. That's why the dining room table has that pine stick in the one corner. Henry got the good leg. I believe Auntie Em left Henry's work leg there so he'd always be at the table.

Now, the real artist in the family is our Auntie Em. Her medium is food and her studio is her kitchen. Whatever Uncle Henry provided as a medium, in a gesture was transformed, teased, poached, or pickled. "If you leave here hungry, it's your own fault." Pickled everything. "If you don't see it on the table, you don't need it." If Henry could cut it off, Auntie Em could pickle it. "Don't ask for what you don't see, it's good training for later in life."

There was a cross-stitched plaque that hung over Auntie Em's stove called, "Recipe for a Good Marriage." It read: "A cup of love, A tablespoon of kindness, And a heaping helping of luck, patience, grace." I'd ask, "Is that poem about you and Henry?" "Ha!" she'd laugh. "Right. When monkeys fly." Aunt Em and me hardly ever spoke. This recipe seemed so out of place in the quiet, desolate world. Yet there it was, like a wish or a prayer. Maybe it covered a hole in the wall. Some kind of hole. Personally, I think we are all made up of the same ingredients. It's the proportions that make us different.

(TOTO BARKS.)

SCARECROW: What, Toto? Don't interrupt. Well, what is it?

TOTO: You're coming to a good part. It's about me.

DOROTHY: Dear Diary, Today I saw Auntie Em sneak bits of turkey to the dog in the kitchen. Uncle Henry would've had a fit. He called Toto livestock. Auntie Em gives out her love like that turkey, a little at a time, and you have to look quick or you miss it. Sometimes at night she comes into my room and tells me stories of faraway places. Like a good farmer planting a seed for an imagination.

And there are the nights I awake screaming in pain, "Scarecrow on fire, Scarecrow on fire." Ever since my trip to Oz I am visited frequently by severe headaches. I call them "Scarecrow on fire" because they're in my brain and they burn so. Auntie Em holds me tight and sings, and I sing along until the pain is gone. She says singing can distract pain. She says if they get any worse she'll take me to see a specialist in Wichita. I ask, "What's a specialist, Em?" She says, "Someone who works on people who are special, like you." "I see. They're like the Wizard." "Yes, like your Wizard."

Em is known far and wide for her ability to see into the future. She says when I get older I will leave the farm because after what I'd seen in Oz a farm would never be able to hold a girl like me. "Will I get married, Em?" She says, "A fella would be lucky to have you, but make sure he's a good one and treats you right. If he don't, you come back to Em. I'll teach you how to do without." "Yes, ma'am." I hug her tight. She touches my hair. "I love you, Auntie Em." "I love you, Dorothy."

SCARECROW: Toto, where is Dorothy now?

TOTO: Keep reading. See? Right there. This part is sad, but then really good.

DOROTHY: Today my dear Toto died. I picked out one of his pups and said, "This one, Em. He's Toto. Just look at him. Toto Two." I worry about Em without Henry. It's hard to make ends meet. I've decided tomorrow I'll take the money I won in that beauty contest and go to Wichita. I'm so very excited. Hopefully I can make something of myself and help Em stay on the farm. I also hope the change will help with my headaches. The Scarecrow has really been burning lately. One day I'll return home. I know there's no place like it. Until then, I know Em will watch Toto Two.

TOTO: There, see? She went to Wichita.

SCARECROW: Wichita. What is a Wichita?

TOTO: It's a city.

SCARECROW: Where there is a city, there will certainly be a wizard. I'll impress on him the nature of my visit, and I'm sure he will help find Dorothy. Which way to Wichita?

TOTO: Follow the gravel road. Watch out for trucks and cars and tractors. That's what got Toto Number One. We Totos tend to run into traffic.

SCARECROW: Trucks and cars and tractors, oh my.

The little dog barked and ran away. Follow the gravel road. Follow the gravel road.

WIZARD: This is WOOZ, the heart, mind, and spirit of the prairie. We've come to the conclusion of this broadcast. Dorothy, would you take us out with a song?

Song: "Somewhere over the Rainbow"

Act II

Song: "Wreck of Me" (with video)

SCARECROW: Excuse me, excuse me. Which way to Wichita?

DRY GOODS MAN: What?

SCARECROW: No, which?

DRY GOODS MAN: Which what?

SCARECROW: Which way?

DRY GOODS MAN: How's that?

SCARECROW: Which way?

DRY GOODS MAN: To where?

SCARECROW: Wichita?

DRY GOODS MAN: What?

SCARECROW: No which?

DRY GOODS MAN: Which what?

SCARECROW: Wichita.

DRY GOODS MAN: What?

SCARECROW: This could take a while, couldn't it?

DRY GOODS MAN: Yeah, it usually does.

SCARECROW: Okay, look. I need that radio. It's the key to finding Dorothy.

DRY GOODS MAN: Sure, I got a whole room full of 'em. The feller that sold 'em to me came into town had a big show with people playing music and singing, broadcast it, then he drove away with the tower. Left me with a pile of radios and nothing to listen to. Every once in a while he parks outside of town. He must be out there somewhere or got a taller tower.

SCARECROW: I see. It's amazing, isn't it? Like magic, Kansas people find machines to help with everything—the labor, travel, even thoughts.

NEWSPAPER MAN: Radio ain't magic. It's called a medium.

SCARECROW: Like a magician?

DRY GOODS MAN: No, it's called a medium because it ain't rare or well done.

SCARECROW: I think in time there will be a radio in every home to do all the heavy thinking for people and free their time for dreaming, like a prosthetic intelligence for the weak of thought.

DRY GOODS MAN: Hmmmm, I'll tell you what, Scarecrow. You help me straighten out these books, and I'll give you a radio.

SCARECROW: Now, the thing about accounting is, if there is a problem, then there will be an anomaly, something out of place. Even chaos viewed in retrospect reveals patterns. Follow the pattern, find the anomaly, a break in the . . .

Ahhhh, here! I said, pointing to a name. This is your man. He's the embezzler.

The man reading the newspaper looked up.

NEWSPAPER MAN: I gotta be going.

SCARECROW: Oh, it's him, he was the embezzler. Corrupted no doubt by the alphabet. Chalk up another one for numbers.

Steve Yoakam, who played the Lion, the Wizard, and five other roles, with Simone Perrin, who played Dorothy. (TOM CAMPBELL)

Dan Chouinard, who played the Tin Man, the Newspaper Man, and Toto Two, too. (TOM CAMPBELL)

Cellist Michelle Kinney and the *Scarecrow* cast: Dan Chouinard, Steve Yoakam, Simone Perrin, and Kling. Silent film from a 1910 production of "The Wizard of Oz" played on the back wall of the theater. (TOM CAMPBELL)

House of Mercy Band: Jon Olson, Doug Trail-Johnson, Angie Talle, Page Burkum (drums, obscured), C. P. Larson, Dave Strahan. (TOM CAMPBELL)

After the fight was over I had a radio . . . and a town named Wichita . . . and a tailwind. The next day, full of fresh straw and a new paint job, I started off. This was the best I'd felt about finding Dorothy since I'd landed in Kansas.

WIZARD: We have a real treat for you tonight. She was such a hit the last time we had her on. It's been awhile, but we finally found her.

DOROTHY: Hello, Wizard.

WIZARD: Hello, Dorothy. Now last time we had you on, you had just won a contest.

DOROTHY: Lot's happened since then, Wizard.

WIZARD: Is that so?

DOROTHY: Was I still on the farm?

WIZARD: Yes, with your Auntie Em.

DOROTHY: Dear Em. She said the farm would never hold me, and how true that came to be. I lit out, determined to take Kansas like a twister. Leave a trail a mile wide.

WIZARD: Well, that's a horse of a different color. How did that work out for you?

DOROTHY: Sometimes when you fall in love, falling for the sake of falling, it doesn't really matter who you land on. It's like shopping when you're hungry. Chances are, you're not going to make the best choices.

WIZARD: There's truth in that.

DOROTHY: Well, he was Mr. Wrong. Everything Kansas wasn't, and I liked everything about that.

WIZARD: A dangerous type. Oh, no.

DOROTHY: But, Wizard, in my defense, there's something irresistible when something a bit feral falls for you.

WIZARD: I see.

DOROTHY: But there's also the carelessness.

WIZARD: Love thrives in audacity and perishes in carelessness.

DOROTHY: He was careless until I could care less. So you know what I did?

WIZARD: What?

DOROTHY: I stayed. Stayed with him. I know, but I didn't know what to do. I couldn't go home. Not yet. I was afraid. That's it. But sometimes a body will do what the mind will not. A fever took me.

WIZARD: It took more than you, Dorothy. It was a fire.

DOROTHY: The worst one yet. Fear got to the white-hot. Sometimes I wonder if he died in the fire. Or why didn't I throw water on him. Throw water on him? I know better than to throw water on a witch. Whatever the truth, what's past is past. So I was put away for a spell. When I got out, he was gone. That's when I started looking for you. I knew the Wizard, the Wizard will know what to do.

WIZARD: You always have a home here with us.

DOROTHY: Thank you. There's really no place like it. I feel better already.

Song: "Trouble Comin'"

LION: (*ROARS.*) What kind of world is this that cages wild animals? I mean, what part of "wild" don't you understand? I need to find Dorothy.

Two weeks later, I was sold to the Carson Brothers Circus, Freak Show, and Menagerie. One day a man came into my cage. He carried a whip and a side arm. He had a key on a long chain, and he used it to unlock my door. I said, "Dorothy, she's in trouble." *Crack*. He cracked a whip. The smell of fear on him was overbearing. In the wild, a fearful animal is the most dangerous. Unpredictable. Can't be reasoned with. *Crack*. He came at me with a chair. A chair? Come on. A chair. So I gave him a little roar; you know, "Get out of my space." Oh, he liked that. *Crack*. I roared louder. He loved that. "Hut hut, yah Simba." *Crack*. I thought, "Well, he's going to really love this." ROAR. *A full-blown knee weakener*. No, no that was too much. He ran out but next day he was back, and over time I learned I wasn't to walk upright or try to speak.

And people came by the hundreds, the thousands. *"See Simba! Lord of the Jungle!"* Of all the lions, I was by far the largest one anyone had ever seen. *"One thin dime, one tenth of a dollar!"* I was getting famous. *"All real! All live!"* I thought hopefully that someday Dorothy would see me. *"Step Right Up!"*

The worst part was the food. Rancid meat every day. Good Glinda, it was bad. There was a girl. She would enter with the trainer. They would place the food in the main cage. One day, the trainer left open the door to my quarters, so suddenly there I was in the cage with her. I was just about to pounce. Then I saw her, up close. It was a mouse. A mouse! And now she stood face to face with certain death. That's when she did something I will not forget as long as I live. She reared up on her hind legs and bared her teeth. It was the bravest thing I've ever seen. Whatever was waiting for her to return was clearly more important than life itself. I knew what to do. I cried, "Please, no!" I wept; I begged for mercy. She took her food and left. Every day she returned. I learned from her that real bravery isn't being unafraid of doing something. No. It's being afraid and doing it anyway.

TIN MAN: It's all so beautiful, really, when you think about it. Love. Love is pure, like an element, at its first stage. That's true, but lasting love is an alloy. In other words, it's simple to fall in love but much more complex to stay aloft in love. That's why Cupid is depicted as a baby. But mature, lasting love is a combination of luck, patience, and grace. And I don't mean grace as some reach beyond the grasp. No, grace as in a touch of the divine, finding the wonder in what is, the here and now. I learned this in a place called Kansas.

I made my way to Wichita through a quick and platonic friendship with a locomotive. And I soon stood before a grand-looking building proclaiming itself a museum. I wondered if it was like my home back in Oz. I could perhaps see how their witches in Kansas lived. Perhaps I could borrow their crystal ball and find Dorothy. Upon entering I found that instead of housing antiquities and witches' paraphernalia, it featured art, painting, sculpture, photographs. Now, I haven't seen art for art's sake. Everything in Oz has a function as well as an aesthetic, so I don't know what I like, but I know it's art.

I found this work fascinating, trying to hold what is ever shifting: beauty, truth, a moment. I was looking at a painting of a woman. It was beautiful in its way, but then a real woman stepped in front of me. She was real and visceral and breathing and warm and alive. Yes, I thought, it's why lives are stories not syllogisms. Why the ancients put the gods in the stars, so they couldn't be captured.

I was so overcome I started crying. Of course, I seized up. Then I realized the woman, I knew her—it was Dorothy! I tried to talk to get her to turn and see me, but I was solid as stone. She walked on, never turning. Oh, love, you've done it to me again. Finally a guard said, "What are you doing in here?" I thought, "Thank heavens. Oil me up so I may finish my cry and find Dorothy." But no, he took me into another part of the museum and placed me among sculptures marked, "D'art Moderne." Here I sat for months under the scrutiny of critics and frustrated art students. Everyone had a comment, most not very flattering at all.

SCARECROW: Wichita is magnificent. Beautiful. I can't imagine there could be a greater city in this entire land. I made my way to the city offices and was stopped by a guard.

MAN: Who are you?

SCARECROW: Please tell the Wizard.

MAN: You mean Mayor.

SCARECROW: Tell the Mayor Wizard that Scarecrow, high regent and defender of the realm of Oz, the present president, poobah, do dah, alpha dog, monarch, high falootin', straw boss, Mr. Know-it-all, honcho, alpha, numero uno, top bale, status quo, hole in one, wizard ad nauseum ad nauseum, hither thither and yon, requests an audience. I'll wait.

The man returned.

MAN: He says who?

SCARECROW: Scarecrow, high regent . . .

MAN: Come back later. He's busy.

SCARECROW: But I've come so far. Tell him I know about the ruby slippers.

MAN: You know about the Ruby Slippers? Well, why didn't you say so? Come on in.

SCARECROW: Once inside, the man turned rather cold.

MAN: So you know about the Ruby Slippers.

SCARECROW: I know many things. Genius is the capacity for knowledge.

MAN: Uh huh. Well, the Ruby Slipper episode, that all happened years ago.

SCARECROW: Yes. I was there.

MAN: You were there?

SCARECROW: He squinted trying to recognize me.

MAN: I see. You're like a conscience?

SCARECROW: I can be.

MAN: The mayor has a good heart.

SCARECROW: I'm sure he does.

The man led me out a back door and into an alley. Suddenly he grabbed me roughly.

MAN: Look. I don't know what you want, but what's past is past and doesn't need somebody like you digging up the Ruby Slippers. He was in that place once, once. Got me?

SCARECROW: Are we talking about the same thing?

MAN: And the girl.

SCARECROW: Dorothy?

MAN: That's the name. They just talked. That was it.

SCARECROW: She clicked her heels.

MAN: There was no heel clicking, got me?

SCARECROW: He began rolling up his sleeves.

MAN: I can see we're going to have to make an example out of you.

SCARECROW: Couldn't I just be a metaphor? Do I have to be an example?

And that's when he tore off my head.

LION: The night the fire broke out, the mouse had just left. I was told later the clown father had fallen asleep smoking a cigar. People were unaware, but the animals knew right away, and I was like everyone. "Help! Save me! Get me out of this cage!" I knew no one was going to let out a lion. Let him burn.

That's when the mouse returned to my cage. The fire moved toward us. She was afraid, I could sense it. I roared, "Get out of here!" She ran away. I thought, "Good. Save yourself." She returned not alone, but with at least fifty mice. One mouse can't do much, but fifty mice is another story. They had with them the trainer . . . rolling him along like a log. Several mice got behind him, lifted him high. "No!" he yelled, far more afraid of these mice than he'd ever been of me. Once the trainer was at the gate, they pulled the key on the chain from his pocket, ran it to the lock, and I was free.

SCARECROW: "Let me go. Let me go," I cried at the man from my detached head, but the guard held me tight. I employed the use of a technique the Lion taught me. It's a roar guaranteed to back off assailants, but to make it my own, I added words. "Mister, you just opened a can of whiplash, balderdash, and sassafras. I'm gonna ride you like a nightmare, peel you like an onion, be in more places than lint. Visit parts of you hitherto known only by food. Stand at attention and salute the general desolation of your private parts. Then bend over and kiss your own horrible end good-bye." Well, it did freeze him briefly. Then I remembered too late the words of the Lion. "You have to be prepared to back it up."

MAN: How are you making your voice come out of that head?

SCARECROW: The man began to pull the straw from me and then threw what was left of me in the mud.

LION: I thanked my friend the mouse and ran as the flames consumed the circus. Unfocused fear is rage, but now I'd seen courage, real courage, and knew there is no courage without brains and heart. So I thought that the Scarecrow would wonder if anyone was still trapped by the fire and the Tin Man would say the right thing to do is save them. Then I would say, "Then let's go, you idiots!" So I had the conversation . . . I wonder . . . the right thing to do . . . let's go, you idiots! I found the lion trainer and pulled him to safety. I saved the dog act, Lobster Boy, Pyro Girl, ouch, the clown family. I kept pulling out clowns like there was no end to them, until we all sat exhausted safely clear of the fire.

TIN MAN: Finally a gifted student visited the museum, saw me, and said, "Hey, I think this tin man is kinetic. It's just seized up." That night, after closing time, the young man returned with a companion. They had with them an oil can, which they applied to my joints. When they got to the jaw I thanked them heartily. The two snuck me into the night and back to their lodgings on campus. I spent the night living among the bohemians. Sharing in their bacchanalian fête, becoming a receptacle at times for various mind-stimulating substances. Their knowledge of horticulture never ceased to amaze me.

SCARECROW: As I lay in the mud, a ragtag human came by at one point and put me on like a coat. It was never going to work ideologically. We differed. He wanted food, I wanted a syllogism. I was left in a trash bin until a kindly woman found me. I was taken and cleaned—first, a good washing, then as I spun in a tumbling dryer I saw, through the glass portal, the Tin Man.

TIN MAN: I was now free to search for Dorothy. As I made my way from campus I passed a laundromat. I knew it would give me great solace to sit among my old friends, the machines. It was a very busy day, all the machines were going. In the cacophony of engines and tumblers, I heard patterns. In the window of the drying machine was a familiar face. It was quite faded and spinning rapidly, but it was undoubtedly the Scarecrow.

SCARECROW: Tin Man set me free. We made our greetings, he cried, then he took some cloth from a lost-and-found bin and stuffed me back into shape. The Tin Man's aesthetics were amazing. He gave me bulging biceps, legs like pillars, a square jaw, quite the physique. Where had he learned this?

TIN MAN: From Michelangelo.

SCARECROW: Michelangelo. In the areas he used synthetic fabric I was quite numb, but luckily he had used wool socks for my head and mouth. "Quickly!" I insisted. "We must make haste. This radio will help." I no sooner turned a knob than,

VOICE: This just in! A fire broke out in the Carson Brothers Circus, and of all things a lion saved the day. A lion, of all things!

SCARECROW: That's got to be our Lion. Come on to the circus! But we have to watch out for trucks and cars and tractors.

TIN MAN: Trucks and cars and tractors, oh my.

LION: After the fire, perception had switched back into my favor. They gave me a medal. I made sure to walk upright. I shaved my mane so I looked like a large orange kitty cat. I learned how to speak another language. *Meow.*

Now to find Dorothy. Suddenly there was a knock at the door and sure as a monkey's got wings, there stood the Scarecrow and Tin Man . . . They looked . . . older.

SCARECROW: My dear, dear friends. This marks an important day, but I must caution us to save our celebration until we find our Dorothy. One for all.

ALL THREE: And all for Dorothy.

LION: Are you stuffed with socks?

SCARECROW: Let's go.

Song: "Ain't the Moon" (with video)

SCARECROW: Look, it's the blinking beacon of truth!

TIN MAN: WOOZ.

WIZARD: Folks, due to the mail we've received at WOOZ, we have Dorothy Gale back with us today.

DOROTHY: Hello, Wizard.

WIZARD: Hello, Miss Gale. What is new with you?

DOROTHY: Well, Wizard, it's rather earthy.

TIN MAN: It's Dorothy!

LION: Let's go.

SCARECROW: No, wait. Let's listen.

WIZARD: That's all right. This is radio. They say there will be restrictions some day, but I doubt it. The airwaves are free to all. It's why I can sell my . . . medicine. Run for office. ANYTHING.

DOROTHY: Well, Wizard, they say you spend the first half of your life running away from home and your second half trying to get back to home.

LION: What are we waiting for? Let's go!

SCARECROW: Shhhh!

DOROTHY: Well, one day, just after we last met, here on your show, I was passing by a place called the Ruby Slippers.

WIZARD: I know it, of it, a tavern.

DOROTHY: That's right.

WIZARD: Den of iniquity.

DOROTHY: I saw a sign. A sign in the window: "Help wanted, inquire within." I thought, "That's brilliant. Of course the answer lies within." I walked inside.

WIZARD: To the lion's den, if you will.

DOROTHY: Yes, and they said actually, the sign meant they were hiring a waitress. Well, this was even better. I was given the job, and in time I became a B-girl.

WIZARD: B girl. Fill in our audience.

DOROTHY: A B-girl sits at the bar and talks with people. That's it. Mostly it's listening. You say, "How interesting" and "Tell me more" and "You can't be serious." It's truly the art of conversation.

WIZARD: Did you enjoy it?

DOROTHY: Not at first. At first I liked my men like my coffee, stupid. Then I realized they just needed to talk. In time I met folks from all walks—farmers, salesmen, even politicians. For a time I had as many women clients as men. I heard it all. See, a place like the Ruby Slippers is full of ghosts, torments and desires looking for a home, memories that go bump in their hearts and minds. I provided a home for those ghosts. Stories. Beautiful. I learned something. Every story is a love story.

TIN MAN: I love a good love story.

SCARECROW: Shhh.

LION: Yeah, shhhh.

WIZARD: Now, Dorothy, this is the time the war broke out.

DOROTHY: That's right. A soldier came in and paid and never said a word. Just sat there. He came in again, same thing. Finally I said, "You know, we can talk."

And he did. Boy, did he. I only knew him for six weeks. See, you learn love by being loved, and every time I saw him I thought of that recipe on Auntie Em's wall. The ingredients for marriage and how he'd met every ingredient, proportion and all. And what usually happens when you follow a recipe? In time there was something in the oven.

WIZARD: He went overseas, didn't he?

DOROTHY: Yes, he did.

WIZARD: Did he return?

DOROTHY: That's not for me to answer. Nobody returns from combat. Those who do just come home to another war.

WIZARD: Tell us about Emily.

DOROTHY: Well, Wizard, she's my daughter and the light of my life. We live on Aunt Em and Henry's farm now. We have a hired hand we call Hired Hand. Not the sharpest tool in the light socket.

WIZARD: Coupla yellow bricks short of a road.

DOROTHY: Exactly. For a hired hand he's . . . "world wise." Helps me with Emily. He'll say, "Raisin' a kid ain't rocket surgery for crying outside. Just give her love." I'll sing to her at night.

WIZARD: To distract the pain?

DOROTHY: Sometimes.

WIZARD: A love song?

DOROTHY: They all are. I'll say, "Emily, when it comes to home there's no place like it. It's wherever you feel loved, and like beauty and truth, home can be a moving target: sometimes hard to hit and other times you could find it with your eyes closed, just click your heels." And I'll say what I say every night. "I love you, Emily," and she'll say, "I love you, Mom."

(Sings slowly, like a lullaby, several lines of "We're Off to See the Wizard.")

WIZARD: Dorothy, are you all right?

Goodnight, Dorothy. Goodnight, all.

SCARECROW: Wizard. Hello, Dorothy, we're here.

WIZARD: Scarecrow, Lion, Tin Man, my dear friends . . . how did you find me?

SCARECROW: We heard you on the radio in the Lion's trailer.

TIN MAN: You said RR2 and double D.

SCARECROW: We've come to find Dorothy.

LION: Take her where she'll be safe.

TIN MAN: Free of pain.

WIZARD: She isn't here. She's gone home. You can catch her if you hurry.

TIN MAN: Let's go!

LION: Come on!

SCARECROW: No, stop!

TIN MAN: But, Dorothy!

SCARECROW: She's gone home. When Dorothy was a girl we gave her direction. A path home. It was larger and more colorful than Kansas, as it needed to be. But now she belongs here with Emily.

TIN MAN: What about us? Where do we belong?

WIZARD: If you're like me, and I know I am, you've found Kansas is a world of ambiguity and only those that can handle change survive.

SCARECROW: It's called "evolution," but I've learned that's a bad word here from a man who served as a good example of why it probably isn't true.

LION: Uh. Now what?

TIN MAN: I know I have a heart. I feel it breaking.

SCARECROW: There never seems to be a tornado when you need one.

WIZARD: I have just the thing—my balloon. I keep it at the fairgrounds. I'd be happy to fly you all back to Oz. It's high time I go back. The change will do me good.

SCARECROW: We made our way to the balloon. Written on the basket a sign that read, "Oz or Bust" and "Objects Closer Than They Appear." It was then apparent that the Wizard had prepared for this all along.

WIZARD: Yes, in Oz I was a fool masquerading as a genius. But here I am quite the opposite.

SCARECROW: A spectacular storm was brewing off in the distance.

WIZARD: We need to beat that weather. Let's go. Hurry!

SCARECROW: The Wizard then climbed in the basket and held on to the rope. Good-bye, Dorothy!

LION: Good-bye!

SCARECROW: Tin Man. Don't cry, you'll seize. Grab him, Lion.

LION: I've got him.

SCARECROW: Suddenly a great gust of wind took the balloon and Wizard high into the air

WIZARD: AAHHHHHH.

TIN MAN: The balloon!

WIZARD: I don't know how to turn this thing around!

SCARECROW: The balloon then flew off with the Wizard, stranding the three of us in Kansas.

TIN MAN: Oh, no. This can't be!

LION: Look!

TIN MAN: It's a twister!

SCARECROW: That cyclone is headed in our direction. I have an idea. Come on, fellas! That's our ticket home. Are you with me?

TIN MAN: Yes, it's the right thing to do.

LION: Then let's go, you idiots!

SCARECROW: We grabbed paw, metal, and straw. And ran headlong into the twister. Good-bye, Dorothy! Good-bye!

DOROTHY: (Sings.) Follow, follow, follow . . .

DOCTOR: Dorothy? Dorothy? Are you all right? Dorothy, it's me, the doctor.

DOROTHY: Where am I?

DOCTOR: You're at the hospital.

DOROTHY: Hospital?

DOCTOR: Yes, in Wichita. We were talking in my office, getting a medical history, and you had a seizure.

DOROTHY: Wizard?

DOCTOR: No, "Doctor."

DOROTHY: I know you.

DOCTOR: Yes, we met long ago. You were a girl and you struck your head. A tornado. That was me. I treated you.

DOROTHY: You put out the fire.

DOCTOR: Yes, that's right.

DOROTHY: I remember now. I thought you were on the radio.

DOCTOR: What? No.

DOROTHY: But when I was a girl you told me you were in radio.

DOCTOR: No, no. I said I was a radiologist. It's like the radio. Waves, invisible, that travel to places we can't see.

DOROTHY: Like Oz.

DOCTOR: Well, now I'm a neurologist. I study the brain.

DOROTHY: Doctor, is there something the matter with me?

DOCTOR: You see, Miss Gale, your brain is made up of several lobes or zones. Each with very specific tasks. It's remarkable, really. The motor skills, breathing, etc., are locked away, hard to reach, hard to injure. The parts that make up personality, they sit right up front. When you hit your head as a girl, you recall that it was back here. The occipital zone.

DOROTHY: Oz.

DOCTOR: Yes, of course. Oz. Well, as a girl you actually damaged the occipital zone. To what extent we don't know, but as we age, injuries from our youth have a habit of reoccurring. This is the area responsible for vision. Hallucinations. In your case, colors may appear more vibrant than ever, and then suddenly, sometimes the world appears black and white.

DOROTHY: It does; it really does.

DOCTOR: And then at times you may be experiencing events that occur only in your mind.

DOROTHY: I know. I felt Oz pulling me.

DOCTOR: Well, yes, we've been worried at some point the hallucinations could become your new reality.

DOROTHY: I love Oz. But I love Kansas, too. Oh my. I think it's better to be one place or another, don't you?

DOCTOR: Yes, yes I do. And it seems for now, we have you here. Hopefully for a long, long time. Dorothy, we need a few more X-rays. Hold still and ignore the man behind the curtain.

SCARECROW: Hi, Dorothy.

DOROTHY: Scarecrow. It's you!

SCARECROW: Actually, I'm the doctor's assistant.

DOROTHY: And the Tin Man.

TIN MAN: Hello, Dorothy. And I'm your nurse.

LION: Put 'em up, put 'em up, put 'em up.

DOROTHY: Lion!

LION: What? I'm a lab tech. I've come to take some blood. Put your arm up.

DOROTHY: No. You—all of you were here—all of you in Kansas, but as my friends from Oz. And you were looking for me.

(They all laugh.)

TRIO: Really. Isn't that something? That girl.

DOROTHY: No, you were. But even from afar you helped me so. You taught me courage to do what needs to be done, and you how to love what's right in front of me and to be curious . . . even if it means sometimes risking having your head torn off.

TRIO: Well, that's rich. How about that. Good Glinda.

DOCTOR: Well, Dorothy, there is someone very real that's been waiting to see you.

DOROTHY: Emily, I'm home. Home. There really is no place like it.

SCARECROW: So Dorothy stayed in Kansas and we went back to Oz. The Lion rarely sits in his recliner, the Tin Man has fallen in love with a Munchkin, and I've started trafficking in the alphabet. Perhaps in time Dorothy will come see us again. I hope so.

Song: "Lead Me on Home" (with video)

SCARECROW: (*As epilogue, during instrumental.*) At times you'll find yourself waiting for growth and other times rushing headlong. It doesn't matter. One day you'll round a corner and in an eyeblink you'll find something is missing, was stolen, is misplaced, is gone. Your heart, a memory, a limb, a person, a promise. An innocence is gone. Suddenly you're on a new path. Some folks won't approve. Some will want the other you. Some will cry that you are gone. But what has happened has happened. We pay for laughter, we pay again to weep. Knowledge isn't cheap. To survive, you must return to your senses. Touch, taste, smell, sight, sound. You must live as verbs, not nouns. With each breath we inhale and exhale, we inspire and expire. Every breath has the possibility to cry or laugh a story or a song. Every conversation is an exchange of spirit. The words ride sweet or bitter over the tongue. Remember that scars are monuments of battles survived. When you're born into loss, you grow from it, but when you experience a loss later in life, you have to grow toward it. A slow move to an embrace. An embrace that leaves you holding tight. The beauty wrapped in the grotesque, an embrace that becomes a dance. Your new dance. A dance home.

End of Play

Notes on
GULLIVER UNRAVELS

It's said the Irish invented satire. My friend Clare Murphy tells an ancient story that dates back to some of their earliest myths—a time when humans and faeries walked the earth together, a time of changelings and Druids and shapeshifters and giants. Clare tells it beautifully, how a new king treats a storyteller poorly and becomes the subject of the teller's newest work. The story places the king in a less than favorable light and is set to a catchy tune, which in no time spreads through the land. The people begin to laugh at the king, he abdicates and flees Ireland. Thus satire is born, a paradox of form: setting humor to deadly serious issues.

Jonathan Swift may be Ireland's most famous satirist, and he's a fascinating paradox of a man: an Irishman with ties to the British Crown, the Dean of the Anglican Church in predominantly Catholic Ireland, a Tory, a true believer in the monarchy, and at the same time a champion of the underclass. He wrote scathing satires against the often oppressive regime he longed to belong to. I came to admire him and feel for the frustration that must have driven his work.

Swift wrote under pseudonyms: Isaac Bickerstaff, MB Drapier. Even *Gulliver's Travels*—more properly, *Travels into Several Remote Nations of the World, in Four Parts, by Lemuel Gulliver, First a Surgeon, and then a Captain of Several Ships*—did not carry his name until several years after his death. He chose to use satire, to cut deep into the hypocrites, putting him at odds with the powerful in a very volatile time. He struggled to balance his personal ambition with his strong moral sense.

Gulliver's story is a timeless piece. There will always be those who believe themselves to be giants, or times we feel small, or notice that science has its head in the clouds or yahoos have moved in next door, or see the solemnity of the equine perspective as far superior to our own. The book can also be an exhaustive read, full of invented facts and figures. It helps to have clues to Swift's exact targets: the cruelty of the aristocracy, an uninformed populace led like sheep. It seems that few from his time were spared a poke from the sharp end of his pen.

In 1998 I had the great fortune of working with Theatre de la Jeune Lune on a piece called "Gulliver: A Swift Journey." It was a beautiful production, a visual feast, and it created in me a need to go further with this character and the lands he explores.

I don't know where to begin with my fascination for Lemuel Gulliver and his creator Jonathan Swift. I do know neither one seemed to question *his* need to satisfy curiosity.

Certainly, when I was a child, a land like Lilliput, with its tiny, crushable adults, seemed like a place I might enjoy. Years later, when I finally sat down and read the entire book, I discovered the other lands Gulliver visits—Brobdingnag, Laputa, Glubbdubdrib, and Japan—and I became more intrigued. Every new land offered a challenge, and Lemuel never quite fit in. He was tiny or big, or the other people lived on theories and floating islands, or they were a race of intelligent horses—or were Japanese.

I have found there are many similarities that connect the world he inhabited to our own: an ever-crumbling superpower struggling to keep the wealth in the hands of the few, a community losing touch with nature, religion concerned more with acquiring souls than saving them. We are obsessed with "what is true," and at the same time we allow opinion to rule our news. It's time to visit Lilliput again.

The Character of Lemuel Gulliver

For me, the dualism of truth and fiction started with George Washington. In grade school, we learned that he could not tell a lie. That was fine, I could understand that through some genetic anomaly or condition passed on by his ancestors, little George was physically unable to fib. But it became confusing when I found out that I was supposed to live under the same "no lie" code, even though my genes allowed—no *encouraged*—me to lie. Not only could I lie, but I had profound aptitude and a clear, bright future in the industry.

I'm sure the first five sentences I ever uttered included "Wasn't me," "He did it," and "Yes, that's mine." So while George's condition was favored and praised, because of a slim, unfortunate difference in DNA, I was sent to the principal's office, tasted soap, and was forced to say "I'm sorry" on a daily basis.

Luckily, after years of treatment and dedication, I have come to a point in life where I never lie or adjust the truth in any manner. The stories I tell can be taken at face value: the villains are as evil and impure as described, and the heroes are as virtuous and pure as I have proven witness.

There is a third category of story that combines truth and fiction, an impossible or seemingly impossible tale delivered in such a manner that makes its plausibility moot. There are experts among us who spin yarns from invisible fibers, the masters of the pseudo-canard, those who boldly test the elasticity of the waistband of truth. A genuinely gifted's recitation, though farfetched beyond reason, is delivered with such conviction, passion, and grace that no one ever calls them on it. Rather, we revel in the teller's ability to extol, expound, and explain never-before-revealed "facts" and third-, fourth-, and fifth-hand accounts with a straight face and full conviction. Some people are frustrated by these souls, but if you are able to give yourself over to their parallel logic, you will be rewarded with a journey worth recounting and revisiting. For with a good liar, there's a tear in every joke and a bit of truth in every canard. My feeling is, most truth has a shelf life, anyway, so let's just open it up and have at it before it spoils on its own.

Over the years I've learned to seek out these fact wrestlers, characters from the past and present who represent the best in spurious verbosity. Those like Shakespeare's Falstaff, bigger than life, especially in his own mind, and Don Quixote, on crusade with his fabricated existence. The secret club that traffics in the paradox of what we believe and what we'd *rather* believe. Perception and reality must always hang in the balance. I've found the best of the best have fallen for the story themselves, those so steeped in craft even a lie detector test would not unearth the damage they've done to the truth.

These conjurers have us begging for more, create an appetite for fresh untruths, and like any addict, we crave ever increasing doses, ever expanding boundaries in the terrain of what is for sure.

For the stage I wanted to create a Gulliver that I could meet, flesh and blood, so a friendship could grow. At the same time, I wanted him to be someone larger than life, someone who could say the most outlandish things and make them believable. He must also hold an innocence, a curiosity that gives credibility to his most fantastic encounter. Suddenly I realized I already knew this person. I knew three of him.

His name is Bil Lepp. Bil Lepp is a brilliant storyteller who has won the West Virginia liars contest five years in a row. He's also an ordained minister, and he assures me the two are not mutually exclusive. When Bil read "He lieth in green pastures," he took it to heart and way beyond the green pastures.

His name is Steve Kramer. In the eighties, when the Twin Cities were an amazing place to be twenty and immortal, Steve was the lead singer/songwriter for a group called the Wallets, their music like a cross between *Mad Magazine* and Beethoven. In 2011, Tony Bol from the Fitzgerald Theater put us together to create a show called *Of Mirth and Mischief.* So to get it going, we agreed to meet on a Monday morning at a local coffee shop. I was waiting there when Steve entered in usual boisterous Kramer fashion. The whole place turned to see what the commotion was and found Steve staring back at them. Allowing a brief pause, he then announced, "I'm from the home office, and you're all fired." The place was stunned—then broke out in cheers.

We met every Monday for coffee.

One day Steve said to me he loved bird watching, and so does my wife Mary. So she signed them up for a bird-watching class. There are two energies that happen when bird watching: disturbance and awareness. You start with disturbance and eventually merge toward awareness. Steve kind of stayed in part one. Mary said most of the teacher's time was spent undoing some of Steve's information. At one point she overheard him telling a girl, "I guess eagle eggs are the size of beach balls."

Goethe said people should go to the theater like they were visiting a foreign country, open to new experiences and reveling in connections. This is how Steve entered a room. For the show at the Fitzgerald, I soon figured out that my job was to get us to the next song.

We had a meeting early on where Steve told everyone he thought it would be great to drop thousands of ping pong balls on the audience. Tom Campbell, the production manager, looked up and said a single word. "No." Steve said that he'd already ordered the ping pong balls. "Absolutely not." After the meeting, I told Steve, "Sorry, Steve, you already ordered all those ping pong balls." He said, "That's okay, I mostly wanted them to see what they came in." He used some of his ping pong balls to make a pair of shoes.

Steve embodied Shakespeare's phrase connecting the lover, the fool, and the poet in imagination, all one.

His name is Steve Kelly Kling, my brother. My brother is adept at bending and stretching the truth, or making the truth sound like a lie and a lie like the truth. One time we were having a few frosty ones at a nearby bar. A gentleman joined us and began talking about his amazing car. He said it had never been beaten in a race and went on to explain in great technical detail why this was so. He closed by challenging anyone in the bar who would care to race: he would gladly match any wager.

My brother took the bet.

My brother then said, "On one condition—that I get to choose the distance."

The man asked, "What kind of car do you have?"

My brother said, "I drove my pickup truck, but that's beside the point. I don't need a car. I will outrun your car on foot."

The man almost coughed up a lung laughing. "You're going to outrun my car on foot?"

"That's right," said my brother. "On foot. My bet is five dollars."

"I'll take it," says the man, "let's go."

We made our way to the parking lot. The street was cleared. The two combatants made their way to the scratch line.

As they lined up, my brother said, "Ten feet."

"What?" shouted the man.

"Ten feet," repeated my brother. "The distance of the race."

"Ten feet?"

"On your mark, get set, go."

The two took off. The car never had a chance. My brother beat him by over half the distance. Took the five dollars and bought us a couple more beers. He succeeded in leaving the truth intact and proving sometimes a tall tale can be one hundred percent non-fiction.

So this is my Gulliver: the verbosity of Lepp, the good-hearted curiosity of Kramer, and the audacity of my brother.

Is Gulliver a liar? My opinion is no . . . and yes. I think Gulliver has the Washington gene, but the conviction he holds may not be the same for another. Are his stories true? Yes . . . and no. Like good myths, there are truths deeper than the facts. Swift said that the sin of a lie didn't live in the words but in the intent. If the sin of a lie is at its intent, then it seems the virtues of a canard could likewise be argued.

Does Lilliput exist? Just because we haven't seen it, that doesn't mean it doesn't exist.

Besides, Lemuel Gulliver has been there and can tell you all about it. It starts like this:

> There is a neighborhood bar I frequent. It's pretty quiet—people go there to be with other people, but not to talk with them.
>
> One night, a man comes into the bar and begins to drink. The more he drinks, the more he talks, and the more he talks, the more articulate he becomes. Now, most of us believe this is true about ourselves, but with Gulliver, it's actually the case. He changes from a boorish yahoo into an impressive, eloquent, engaging doctor.
>
> He begins to tell us of a voyage, a voyage to a land we have dreamed of but did not believe in—but in fact, it does exist, and he has seen it and will relate its amazing, unique topography and population—but first will need another drink.
>
> A drink appears, then disappears, and he begins . . .

The Bar

The setting is a bar.

Bars like this one are all across this country, and they're all pretty much the same. Mismatched furniture, cancelled checks taped to the side of the cash register, behind the rail a young bottle of whiskey and a jar of pickled eggs old enough to vote. Signs proclaim "Sorry we're open," and "If assholes could fly, this place would be an airport," and "If you drive your old man to drink drive him here." The restroom doors are labeled "Pointer" and "Setter." This is the kind of bar where you don't want to wear your good shoes.

Bars like this tend to house people from the wide end of the economic pyramid, gathered for solidarity, conversation optional, often found staring into their drinks like ice fishermen waiting for a bite. A bar where hardly a word is spoken because the bartender knows what everyone wants and everyone knows what it costs. These bars are designed more for the incubation of great ideas than the actual hatching.

Bars like this are full of ghosts, people, memories, things that can't find a home, that go bump in our hearts and minds. As Tom Waits says, no one brings anything small into a bar around here.

This place is an amalgamation of the bars from my past:

Taverns I remember as a child, where I sat out in the car while my dad ran in for a quick bump.

Dick's Bar, in my home town, where I had my first drink. Dick's Bar also sponsored our softball team, a team of future accountants and thespians. Our team record was 0 and 2. 0 and 2 years. We never won a game.

Then the Nicollet Bar in St. Peter, when I was in college, where buddies and I held court, talking big, and where I learned your night before was only as good as your ability to tell about it.

The Uptown Bar in Minneapolis. My first job was down the street at the chow mein noodle factory, where they called me "college boy" because I could read. When I first started going to the Uptown, there were B-girls sitting on stools at the bar. B-girls are from a time gone by: women, most in middle age, who sit at the bar and, for a few dollars and a drink, will tell you how smart you are. There are times when it's impossible to resist their art of conversation. That's as far as it goes, but that can be quite a journey.

If you needed something more, next door was Barbie's Sauna, where it was said for twenty bucks you could get anything except Barbie or a sauna.

One time a B-girl told me, "I like my men like my coffee . . . stupid."

This is the kind of bar I imagine Gulliver wandering into. But hanging on the wall, next to the year-round Christmas decorations, the one trophy never inscribed, and the dusty deer head, is something that sets this bar apart. It's a hand-carved ship, set to scale, from the 1700s, when Britannia ruled the seas. Clearly a labor of love, the ship is detailed with working rigging, cannons, and sails. Although it's over a thousand miles from the nearest ocean, it serves as a reminder and at times a vehicle to take patrons far from cares, from land-locked woes and obligations. Directly beneath the ship is a large mounted fish, a northern pike. It looks like a monster attacking the ship, providing both a sense of adventure and a caution that below still waters, tragedy lurks.

One night a stranger came into the bar. He had a t'ick accent . . .

Mrs. Gulliver

She says that it's true, she waits for him to come home after each voyage. When he returns, he has been altered in some way, after Lilliput believing himself to be a giant in constant fear of stepping on townsfolk, one time believing he could talk to a horse. Mrs. Gulliver begins to wonder as the ship slips from the pier: Who will return? Will it be the man she loves? Or will they have to start all over again?

In 2001 I was in a severe motorcycle accident and was unconscious most of the following week. It was touch-and-go for a while. The extent of physical consequences were to be determined, but certainly I had sustained spinal damage and brain injury.

I think of Mary at that time, like Mrs. Gulliver, wondering who would return from this journey. It takes a rare strength, one we can't know until it's called upon, to usher another back into a new life. Mrs. Gulliver represents a slim part of the text, yet even in her brief appearance, she leaves a profound impression. I think Mrs. Gulliver is going to get a bit more voice in the stage version than she is given in the book.

A poem for Mrs. Gulliver

I'll send you my kisses as birds
Hoping they migrate to you
I'll send you my kisses because
By keeping them at home I might tame them

I'll send you my tears on the sea
Hoping they will be lost
I'll send you my tears because
By keeping them at home they might tame me

I'll set my love on the wind
At your back
With kisses and tears my love I'll send
Hoping you'll turn and breathe me in

At "For Love of Annie," a benefit held at the Dakota in Minneapolis, 2011,
for photographer Ann Marsden, who passed away in 2012. (TOM SANDELANDS)

Backstage at *Mirth and Mischief.* (ANN MARSDEN)

CAPE CLEAR

FROM *FOR THE BIRDS*

Cape Clear Island lies off the southernmost tip of Ireland. In many ways, it has the feel of a typical Irish countryside. Whitewashed cottages with thatched roofs, roads not wide enough for two cars to pass, thick hedgerows and rock walls dating back hundreds of years. On the highest point of this tiny island, there are ancient ruins, rock formations, spires and sanctuaries that align the landscape with the stars, like similar structures in South America and Mongolia. At night, Cape Clear unleashes a view of the heavens unlike any other.

In the Cape Clear pub, Jerry, a man from Limerick, decides we should be friends.

The next day Jerry is taking me to have ice cream. As we walk along the road, we are surrounded by a most disturbing sound. It's the birds. Cacophony of calls, whistles, chirps, cackles. Jerry explains that because of Cape Clear's location, birds from all of the major flyways come here. Africa, Europe, North America, even Asia. Blown off course, this is the first land they see. After being blown across the ocean, these birds have decided, "That's it, I'm not going back out there," and have made it home. Cape Clear is an ornithologist's paradise. I see parrots, sparrows, crows, hawks, robins, and so many more that I don't know.

The ice cream is made by a local man who is a blind goat herder. Incredible. Chocolate or vanilla, that's all he makes, "and be careful," says Jerry, "every once in a while, a small stone."

The birds outside are particularly active. The goat herder smiles. We have to almost shout to be heard. I'm reminded of a friend, back in the States.

He has perfect pitch. You hear a car horn honk, he can tell you what key it's in. He is also a Christian, is blind, schizophrenic, and gay. He said years ago his head was so conflicted he thought several times of suicide. Then one day he was in a laundromat. All the machines were going, washers and driers. Inside that chaotic laundromat he could hear patterns. He figured if there were patterns, connections, in that place, there must be in his conflicted life as well.

I sit in the goat herder's shack.

The goat herder smiles, and Jerry looks at me with those intense eyes of his. I'm being given a gift. I don't understand it yet, but I do know:

Sometimes life gives you answers before the question.

STAR TWO

In my time among the constellations
I've found there are families that share my blood and families I'd give my
    blood

I found that Love thrives in audacity
Dies in carelessness
And hides in simple gestures

Knowledge is acquired
Wisdom is recognized
And every good story is a love story

I've learned anger is a tool
Truth has a shelf life
And opposable thumbs are highly overrated

I've learned to dance with the scars
And to Kindly rely on the strangeness of others

I've learned you can't lie to a horse
And when you tell a wiener dog "no," it hears "try another way"

I've learned there's the trip you plan, and then there's the trip you take
And when an angel arrives, sometimes it's to wrestle

I've found that Home has gone from a place that *is,*
to one I remember, to one I create

Where the music makes me dance
I get the jokes
and know which parts are edible

Where I understand the language
Spoken and unspoken
The names of the gods
The heroes
A safe place to grieve
Or to laugh

And that I will meet you there

So I'm sitting on my father's knee.
    I know now, when I reach to the stars, that some of them, though not burning any longer, still send their light. I'm reaching at once to the past and to the future, I'm reaching for home as the sparks fly into the galaxy.
    And somewhere between where I sit and where they send their light, we meet, me looking to the heavens and the stars looking down at what it's like to be alive.

Under the lights in a late-night "Naughty Tales" performance at the Village of Tales
Ojai Storytelling Festival, Ojai, California, 2012. (DEAN ZATKOWSKY)

ACKNOWLEDGMENTS

21A was originally produced by Quicksilver Stage, Minneapolis, in 1984. Its professional regional premier was at The Actors Theater of Louisville in 1985 under the direction of Frazier Marsh. An Off-Broadway debut followed in 1986 at the Westside Arts Theater, Ray Gaspard Artistic Director, under the direction of Steven Dietz.

Director . . . Steven Dietz
Cast . . . Kevin Kling
Taped Voices . . . Kathryn O'Malley and Jaime Meyer
Scenic Designer . . . Michael Sommers
Costume Designer . . . Lori Sullivan
Lighting Designer . . . Jaime Meyer

The Ice Fishing Play was originally produced by the Humana Festival, Actors Theatre of Louisville, Louisville, Kentucky, in 1993.

Director . . . Michael Sommers

Cast
Voice of Tim . . . Fred Major
Voice of Paul . . . Ray Fry
Ron . . . Kevin Kling
Shumway . . . Pepper Stebbins
Francis . . . Victor Gonzales
Irene . . . Susan Barnes
Duff . . . Michael Kevin
Junior . . . William McNulty
Young Ron . . . Collin Sherman

Scenic Designer . . . Paul Owen
Costume Designer . . . Toni-Leslie James
Lighting Designer . . . Karl E. Haas
Sound Designer . . . Darron L. West
Stage Manager . . . Debra Acquavella
Assistant Stage Manager . . . Amy Hutchinson
Dramaturg . . . Julie Crutcher

The Ice Fishing Play was then produced by the Jungle Theater, Minneapolis, in 1994.

Director . . . Michael Sommers

Cast
Voice of Tim . . . Kevin Kling
Voice of Paul . . . Bain Boehlke
Ron . . . J.C. Cutler
Shumway . . . John O'Donoghue
Francis . . . Greta Schwerner
Irene . . . Ann Kellogg
Duff . . . Stephen D'Ambrose
Junior . . . William Francis McGuire
Young Ron . . . Dylan Thuras

Scenic Designer . . . Michael Sommers
Technical Director/Set Construction . . .
  Joe Skala
Costume Designer . . . Amelia Breuer
Lighting Designer . . . Wm. P. Healey
Sound Designer . . . Scott Edwards
Stage Manager/Dramaturg . . . Patricia Fox
Dramaturg . . . Sarah Falls
Mural . . . Laura Hohanshelt, Mike Pittman

Scarecrow on Fire, radio play, was originally produced by the Fitzgerald Theater, Minnesota Public Radio, St. Paul, in 2010.

Director . . . Peter Rothstein

Cast
Scarecrow, Doctor's Assistant . . . Kevin Kling
Dorothy . . . Simone Perrin
Tin Man, Newspaper Man, Toto Two,
  Nurse . . . Dan Chouinard
Lion, Dry Goods Man, Guy, Man, Wizard,
  Doctor, Lab Tech . . . Steve Yoakum

Band . . . House of Mercy
Cello . . . Michelle Kinney

Producer . . . Tony Bol
Producer . . . Stephanie Curtis
Stage Production . . . Tom Campbell
Stage Production . . . Alan Frechtman
Lighting Design . . . Mike Wangen
Sound Design . . . Dan Zimmermann
Stage Production . . . Erin Coscio
Film Archivist & Editor . . . Elizabeth Winter
Coordinating Producer . . . Bethany Barberg
Fitzgerald Theater General Manager . . .
  Ellie McKinney

Thanks to Minnesota Public Radio, the Fitzgerald Theater, L. Frank Baum, Bain Boehlke, Yasha Bol, John Bolding, The Bush Foundation, Karen Casanova, Fred Desbois, Michael Dixon, Rob Gardener, Lowell Gemsey, Steven Griffith, Dr. Jon Hallberg, Dave Harrington, Heart of the Beast Puppet and Mask Theater, Illusion Theater, Mason Jennings, The Jerome Foundation, Jon Jory, Jungle Theater, Jeff Kamin, Steven Kramer, Bill Levis, The McDowell Colony, The McKnight Foundation, Metro Transit, Bonnie Morris, The Playwrights' Center, Michael Robbins, Chris Schodt, Susan Schulman, Joe Sedlachek, George Sutton, Theatre de la Jeune Lune, Michelle Volansky.

Thank you for the research, reading, editing, and care put into this book by the amazing Ann Regan and Mary Ludington. To the wonderful team at the Minnesota Historical Society Press: Pam McClanahan, Shannon Pennefeather, Dan Leary, Robin Moir, Mary Poggione, and Alison Aten. Thanks for the archival help from friends Bonnie Morris and Loren Niemi. Special gratitude to the productions and performers who have brought these characters to life. And to Tony Bol, heart and art.